Did God or Satan Ordain Medical Doctors?

(Ask Huck Finn and/or Nigger Jim: because neither Tom Sawyer nor Judge Thatcher would Know!)

By
The Worldwide People's Revolution!®

Book 022B ♥ ♦

Copyright Dedication and Introduction

By our Selected King's Chief Editor —
Dr. Samuel Walker Edison, Ph.D., M.A., BS, and QC!

ISBN — 13: 979-8669-7719-42

00-01 [_] This Inspired Book is COPYRIGHTED 2015—4017 ADR (After Death and Resurrection) by the Selected King of "The Worldwide People's Revolution!" (A Comprehensive Plan for Obtaining Worldwide Law, Order, Obedience, Peace and True Prosperity!) By The Worldwide People's Revolution!® Book 108, who is the Blest Author of more than 364 Inspired Books, which Speak with both your Head and Heart, if you are not Spiritually Dead, even as many People are, nowadays, who cannot Relate with the Sufferings of other People, who have little Empathy for them, who are, in Fact, beyond any Help: beCause of being "Drugged Out of their Minds," you might say. All Rights are Reserved for their Sakes. No Portion of this Unique Book shall be Reproduced and Sold without Written Permission from **The Worldwide People's Revolution!®**. However, with that Permission, anyone in the World may Reproduce and Sell this Book for a Reasonable Profit, as well as any other Literature by our Selected King, and keep 90% of the Net Profits for their own Prosperity: beCause our Selected King only wants 10 percent of the Net Profits for the Construction of "The Great World TEMPLE of PEACE!" (The Glory of Jerusalem Arises Again in the Great State of Flexible Texas!) By The Worldwide People's Revolution!® Book 017B, which will be the Tallest and Largest Building in the whole World!

00-02 [_] This Special Book is now DEDICATED to the Masses of Ignorant People in this World of Woes, who Suffer with Various Ailments: beCause of being Born and Raised in the Darkness of Ignorance, who do not even know that there are Natural Cures for whatever Ails us, who Vainly Imagine that "Health Care" begins and ends with "Prescription Drugs," who have been "Sold Down the River into Drug Slavery," as Huck Finn might say it, who would most Definitely Capitalize SLAVERY: beCause of being Friends with

"Nigger Jim," in *The Adventures of Tom Sawyer,* and in *The Adventures of Huckleberry Finn,* by Master Mark Twain, who was America's Most-Famous Author and Humorist, who would Naturally Know all about that Slavery: beCause he Lived with it, whereby a Person is FORCED to Say and Do Things that he or she would not Naturally Want to Say nor Do. However, it is one Thing to be made a Slave by some Slave Master (Tyrannical or not), and another Thing to make yourself into a Voluntary Education Slave, Work Slave, Tax Slave, Insurance Bills Slave, Rent Bills Slave, Home-owner Slave, Interest Slave, Mortgage Slave, Transportation Bills Slave, Repair Bills Slave, Food Bills Slave, Water Bills Slave, Gas Bills Slave, Sex Slave, Doctor Bills Slave, Hospital Bills Slave, Drug Bills Slave, Childcare Bills Slave, Nursing Home Bills Slave, Funeral Home Bills Slave, and/or Various other Kinds of SLAVES: beCause of being DECEIVED, while even Imagining that you are FREE, Healthy, and HAPPY, when in Fact you are just another SLAVE of whatever Kind or Color, who might even be in a Worse Condition than Huck Finn or Nigger Jim, who might be Ignorant; but, they are not STUPID, like many "Modern Deceived SLAVES!" (10 Simple Steps for Liberating ALL Modern Slaves, Worldwide, Including Yourself!) **By Liberty and Justice for ALL!** Book 113, who put their Trust in Medical Doctors to Save them from whatever Ails them, rather than Seek the Truths that might Liberate them from their numerous Prisons of Lies, Debts, Worries, Fears, and Self-inflicted Torments! For Example, Americans Waste more than 4 Trillion Dollars per Year on so-called "Health Care," which all Wild Animals Enjoy for FREE! ‡

00-03 [_] I Swear to God that I have no Idea what you are Talking about, O Doctor Samuel Walker Edison. Moreover, I have no Idea WHY in the World you would Capitalize so many of your Uninspired Multiple-Meaning Words, such as Prisons of Lies! What is that all about? †§‡§§

00-04 [_] What are the little Swords and Squiggly Marks (†§‡§§) Representing? Moreover, why is each Verse Numbered the way it is with a Box [_]?

00-05 [_] Well, my Potential Friend, if you Agree with any certain Statement, you should Check the Box with a LARGE GREEN-X MARK; but, if you Disagree with any certain Statement, you should Check the Box with a LARGE RED-X Mark, just to Discover your own Honest Values, about 20 Years from now, just to Discover how much you have Grown Up! For Example, if you Agree with the Sarcastic Statement in Verse 00-03, you should put a Green-X in that Box.

00-06 [_] So, the little Squiggly Section Mark (§) must be Symbolical of a Sarcasm, huh?

00-07 |_| Yes, the Statement is Sarcastic: beCause that Imaginary Person or Unnamed Character does have an Idea concerning almost everything that I state, even if he or she Misunderstands it and also Misinterprets it: beCAUSE of a certain Degree of IGNORANCE. After all, there is not a single Person on this Good Earth who is NOT Ignorant to some Degree, including you and me! Yes, it might be a bit Humiliating to Confess it; but, we are ALL Ignorant about a LOT of Important Subjects, which is a Great Shame on us who Profess to Know something, when we Know nothing yet, as we ought to Know, as the Apostle Paul put it. (See *First Corinthians 8:2*.) Moreover, if we are very PROUD of our Learning, and Imagine that we are very Nolijuboul, just beCause of Learning a few Important Words, that Pride will BLIND our Minds, whereby it will make FOOLS of us: beCause Pride is very Blinding to the Mind, which can be Proven in a Courtroom with Law and Order, which has already been Proven millions of Times by Building Up the PRIDE of the Victims of Military Aggressions, which is WHY all Military "Services" make Sure that they PUFF UP the Pride of their Soldiers, Sailors, and Airmen, and then Award them for Murdering other Innocent Young People, who were also Blinded by their Unjustified Pride. Therefore, all Wise People Choose to Live in a State of Humbleness of Mind, rather than Humiliate themselves with Self-inflicted Pride. Indeed, one cannot be too Humble, nor too Honest, which is the Beginning of True Nolij. Ask George Warmonger Bush and Little Dick Chicanery, if you Doubt it, who have to Live in Shame with their own Consciences as War Criminals, who are a Disgrace to Humanity, whose only Means of Escape from their Guilt is to make Full Confessions of everything, including the False Flag Federal Government Operations of September 11th, 2001. †‡

00-08 [_] So, the Sword (†) must Symbolize something, huh?

00-09 [_] Yes, it Symbolizes the Sword of Controversy, which follows Statements that People might Disagree with: beCause of having a Different View or Perspective concerning all such Statements. Indeed, even the Author might Disagree with such Statements. For Example, a Dimwitcrat (or Deceived Democrat) who Suffers with Chronic Constipation of the Mind, might be Highly Offended with such a Statement as this: beCause of being Guilty of being a DIMWITcrat, even though there are many Democrats who are far more Intelligent and Educated than those Reprobates (Religious Republican Snobs), who just Assume that beCause they "Know God," that they are somehow

Automatically Superior to all other Human Beings: beCause they have been *"Born Again,"* or *"Saved"* from their Sins, in spite of the Fact that they are still Presently Committing Various Kinds of Major SINS, directly or indirectly, which are Transgressions of the Divine Laws of the GODS, who Desperately Need to Study: "The Hopeless Church of Little Faith!" (The Unholy Church of Graceful Sinners, who are Mostly just Liars and Hypocrites!) **By The Good Pastor of Uncommon Sense!** Book 121, which is a Companion Book of: "Which Church is the Right Church?" (Can all Churches be Correct?) **By The Good Pastor of Uncommon Sense!** Book 119! Yes, just to get their Heads Straightened Out, they Need to Study: "The Sixth Book of Moses called GOOD GOVERNMENT!" (The Primary Missing Book in the Holy Bible!) **By The Worldwide People's Revolution!®** Book 126! †‡

A-[_] I Agree.

B-[_] I Disagree. I Believe that there is only ONE God, and she is ALLAH. †§‡§§

C-[_] I Confess that there have been many Gods; but, as for us, there is only one God, who is Jesus Christ. (See *Second Chronicles 13:9—10; Deuteronomy 10:17; Jeremiah 2:11* {"changed" should read "Exchanged"} *11:13; John 10:34—39;* and *First Corinthians 8:5—6,* Gay *King James Version (KJV).*

D-[_] You are a Dimwit: beCause there are 3 Gods — the Father God, the Son God, and the Holy Ghost God. Can you not even Count to 3? Paul listed them. See the References above in the King James Version (KJV).

E-[_] You are not very well Educated with a Capital E. Those 3 Gods are the ONE and ONLY LORD God of Israel, who said, *"Let US make Mankind in OUR Image, according to OUR Likeness,"* which is Proof that they can Count: beCause "us" and "our" are Plural, not Singular. See *Genesis 1:26,* (KJV) for the Proof; and Believe it: beCause it is TRUE. Yes, YOU were Created in the Image of the GODS, and in particular in the Image of the SON of God, who was also the Father of Mankind. †§‡§§ (See *John 5:19, 30; 6:38* {the Sender and the Sent are 2 Different Persons}; *8:16, 18, 28; 12:49—50; and John 14:7— 11, KJV.*)

F-[_] I Fail to Understand all such Confusion. I think that I will skip this chapter.

G-[_] God Help you to Understand that each World must have a Supreme Ruler to Govern it, who is otherwise known as a GOD; and there are Countless Worlds to be Inhabited by the Gods. Therefore, only an Ignorant FOOL would say that there is only ONE God in the Vast Universe. †‡

H-[_] The Holy Spirit tells me that Jesus Christ was the First Man, being the Beginning of the Creation of God in this World. (See *Luke 3:38; Colossians 1:15; 4:16; First Timothy 1:17; 6:16; First John 4:12, 20; Revelation 1:8, 11; and 3:14.*)

I-[_] I say that no Man has seen God at any Time. However, the Bible disagrees with me. Therefore, I am Inconsistent. I cannot help myself. †§‡ (See *John 1:18; 6:46; Exodus 33:20; Deuteronomy 4:12; Genesis 32:30; Numbers 12:8; Exodus 33:11; Deuteronomy 5:4; and 34:10.*) §§

J-[_] Thank Jehovah God that Medical Doctors are not so Inconsistent. Justice Demands that such a Phony, Contradictory God and his Unholy Bible should be brought to Trial! †§‡§§

K-[_] That would not be very Kind of you to put God and the Bible on TRIAL. †§‡

L-[_] Chances are that many Ignorant People will be Lamenting the Day that they Discovered this Judgmental Book. †‡

M-[_] Moneymongers will certainly be Lamenting it, and especially when they are put Out of Business!

N-[_] Not even the most Righteous People will Escape the Judgments of our Selected King, unless they Educate themselves with a Capital E. Indeed, NONE of them will Escape without **"The Swanky Sword of Divine Truths"** on their Sides. †‡

O-[_] Are there no Options? Can we not just Plead Ignorance during the Day of Judgment?

P-[_] I Propose that we get on with the Book, and Discover whether or not God or Satan Ordained Medical Doctors??

Q-[_] The Great Question is this: **"Have we already laid down a Good Foundation of Provable Truths to Build our House of Love on?"** In other Words, are we Prepared to Face the Facts that your Selected King will Present to us, which have Biblical Backing and Logical Proofs? Or, will the Whole Truth Shake Down our Straw Huts and set them on FIRE?? ‡

R-[_] I Resist any Changes. I do not like to Change my Mind about anything: beCause it is Contrary to my Religious Upbringing. Yes, I Believe in Consistency, even if it is Insane! †§‡§§

S-[_] Intelligent Students will Study our Selected King's Inspired Books, so as to have their Swords of Truths very Sharp and Ready to Slice Off the Heads of all Liars! †

T-[_] Time will Prove who is "RIIT," and who is "WRong" — even if it Requires the Great Judgment Day to Prove it. ‡

U-[_] I Understand what you are saying; but, "Right and Rong" are Debatable, and Endlessly so. Indeed, we cannot Prove Exactly what is RIIT, nor WRong. Ask any Pumpkinhead, if you Doubt it.

V-[_] The Victory is to him whose Sword of Truth is Strong and Sharp, who can Withstand any Enemy, including Queen Victoria. †§‡

W-[_] And what in the World does Queen Victoria have to do with Medical Doctors and Warmongers? Was she a Neurosurgeon, or WHAT??

X-[_] X-number of Ignorant People will be "Turned Off" by such Intellectual Trash. I prefer *The Adventures of Tom Sawyer* to *Huckleberry Finn*. Indeed, this is just too Deep for me to Think about it. Please Spare me the Great Mental PAINS of it: beCause Thinking is NOT my "Cup of Tea," as they say. †§‡§§

Y-[_] Well, just Yesterday, I might have Agreed with you; but, not Today: beCause our World Crises have come to a Festering

BOIL, you might say, and the Boil is about to BURST all over us, if we do not Carefully Remove it by Surgery, which will Require some Instrument that is far Sharper than a Sword of Yakety Yak. †‡

Z-[_] The Zeal of our Selected King will make it relatively easy, in spite of your Misspelled Words, Missing Words, Misplaced Words, and Bad Grammar. Just be Patient. Have Faith in ALL that is Good. Be Willing to Prove all Provable Things, and Cling Tightly to ALL that is GOOD: beCause, that is GOD. ‡ (See *First Thessalonians 5:21.*)

00-10 [_] So, the Double Sword (‡) must be Symbolical of the Double-edged Sword of Controversy, which Suggests that it is an Important Subject that should be brought up in a Courtroom, and Specifically at: "The GREAT Worldwide TELEVISED Court HEARING!" (That Great Meeting of the Most-Intelligent and Well-Educated Minds!) By The Worldwide People's Revolution!® Book 041B. For Example, most People would say that there is only ONE God, who is the LORD God of Fathers Abraham, Isaac, Jacob, Joseph, Moses, Joshua, Samuel, Daniel, David, Solomon, Isaiah, Jeremiah, Ezekiel, Joel, Jonah, Jesus, Peter, James, John, and Paul, who were HOLY Men during Biblical Times, who Wrote the *Scriptures* as they were Moved by the Holy Spirit, whose Words of Truths are mostly Ignored by Professing "Christians," Jews, Muslims, Hindus, and Buddhists, alike — all of whom Believe in this God or in that God or in some other Contradictory God, according to their Faith in him or her, whereby they have Produced more than 10,000 Religious Sects with Contradictory Doctrines, whereby they have Invented more than 200 Different Translations of their "Holy Bibles," which they are Unwilling to bring into Courtrooms for TRIALS: beCause they all Know within their Hearts and Minds that all such Books are as Weak as Water, and could never Stand Up in such Courtrooms: beCause of their Weaknesses! For Example, in *Genesis 1:9—10,* in the very first Chapter of the "Holy" *Bible,* it reads: "And God said, Let the waters under the heaven be gathered together into one place, and let the dry *land* appear: and it was so. And God called the dry *land* Earth; and the gathering together of the waters called he Seas: and God saw that *it was* good." — King James Version (KJV). If the Land was in one Place, and all of the Water was in just one Place, why call it "Seas"? {FOOTNOTE: The *Italicized words* in the King James Version were *added* by the Translators, along with Verse Numbers and Paragraphs and Uppercase and Lowercase Letters and even all of the Vowels between the Consonants: beCause Hebrews did not use Written Vowels, which had to be Supplied by the Readers! Therefore, the "Original" Hebrew Version did not use LAND in those Verses. In other words, it would have "red" something like this: "ND GD SD, LT TH WTRS NDR TH HVN B GTHRD TGTHR NT N PLC, ND LT TH DR PR: ND T WS S. ND GD CLD TH DR RTH; ND TH GTHRNG TGTHR F TH WTRS CLD H SS: ND GD SW THT T WS GD," except that it was in Hebrew Chicken Scratches, and each word had 5, 10, 20, 50, or even more than 100 Different Definitions or Meanings to Choose from!} †‡

00-11 [_] God have Mercy! — how in the World did they Manage to Translate all such Gibberish and Chicken Scratchings into ENGLISH, which also has 5, 10, 20, 50, or more than 100 Different Definitions for each Word!? Moreover, the Hebrews spoke almost everything Backwards, like this: "Backwards almost every the Thing was Spoken, moreover." Furthermore, the Hebrews wrote from right to left, and from the bottom of the page to the top of it, in order to make it as Confusing as Humanly Possible! Moreover, when you add in Human Mistakes in Spelling and Grammar, you can easily get a WRong Understanding of the Message, which might even be Coded, or have Sarcastic Figures of Speech, or be Missing Important Words — such as LAND! †§‡

00-12 [_] Well, it is not Difficult for most People to Understand WHY there are more than 200 Contradictory Translations of that Unholy MUTILATED Bible, which is supposed to be *"the Pure Word of the Living God,"* as if there were only ONE Word. Why not call the Bible the *"the Pure Words of the Living God,"* if it is True? ‡

00-13 [_] So, just how True are the Words in the King James Version (KJV)? For Example, if God Actually Gathered ALL of the Water Together into ONE Place, as it states, WHY did he call it the SeaS? Why did he not call it the "Sea"? ‡

00-14 [_] Well, that was beCause the Biblical Gods could not COUNT in the King James Version; but, in other, more Modern Versions, he Learned to Count, and therefore called it the "Sea." {See the *Blue Letter Bible* on the Internet for several Versions, including the *New MAGNIFIED Version (NMV),* which makes the entire Bible Perfectly Understandable from Cover to Cover!} †§‡§§

00-15 [_] Why do you say "Gods," when there was only ONE God, who was the LORD God? Moreover, why did you use 2 of those Squiggly Marks (§§) after that Statement? Is it not Sufficiently Mentally

Tormenting enough to be Sarcastic, without being Doubly Sarcastic? †§‡§§

00-16 |_| Well, if the Statement is so Sarcastic that it Proves itself to be WRong, then that is a very Good Sarcastic Statement, which also contains some Humor, which makes it Special, which is WHY our Selected King's Inspired Books are very Special. For Example, even a Dunce would Know for a Fact that there is no Way to make the Entire Bible Understandable from Cover to Cover, without Adding X-number of Non-original Words, whereby the Bible can be MAGNIFIED. For Example, in *Genesis 1:26,* it reads: And the Gods said, *"Let us make Mankind in our own Image, according to our own Likeness, having Spirits, Minds, and Bodies, whereby each Man will become a Living Soul, even as we are Living Souls: beCause each of the Earths that we have Created will Need Supreme Rulers to Govern them and Manage them Properly, lest they should become Chaotic, Disorganized, and Filled with Confusion, having no Laws nor Rules to Live by; and let them have Dominion over the Fishes in the Seas, and over the Fowls of the Airs, and over the Cattles and all Livestocks, even over all of the Earths, and over every Creeping Thing that Creeps on the Earths, which will Multiply, even as the Stars and Galaxies will also Multiply, so as to be Inhabited by Countless Peoples, who have been Created in the Images of the Gods, so that no 2 Worlds are just Exactly Alike: beCause we Love Diversities, Mysteries, Uniqueness and Perplexities. After all, there is no Limit to our Imaginations. "* So, the Gods Created Mankind in this World in the Image of Yohoovu God, who became the God of the Hebrews, who were Fair and White with Blond Hairs and Blue Eyes, even as Abraham, Isaac, Jacob, Joseph and Moses were: beCause they were God's Chosen People, who were Chosen to Govern this World of Wonders in Righteousness, even before they were Born here. However, without Laws and Rules to Follow, there would be no Way to Do that. †‡ (See *Jeremiah 1:5, KJV.*)

00-17 [_] So, you have ADDED many Words to the Word of God, huh? Is that not a Great SIN, since Moses said that we should not Add anything unto his Words? (See *Deuteronomy 4:2* and Related Verses. Click on TOOLS in the *Blue Letter Bible.*)

00-18 [_] Well, it does Appear that King David and Isaiah also ADDED A LOT of Words to those of Moses, and the Apostle Paul added at least a dozen so-called "Books"! Therefore, if I am Sinning by MAGNIFYING the Truths that were Taught by Moses, then Peter and Paul must have also been Sinning by Adding their Books, huh? †‡ {See:

"Justifications for MAGNIFICATIONS!" (The Problem with Understanding a Complicated Contradictory Mutilated Unholy Bible!) Or: (The Problem with Inventing Lies that are too BIG to DIE!) By The Worldwide People's Revolution!® Book 094.}

00-19 [_] Well, neither Peter nor Paul added any LIES to the Word of God, which was ONE Word, which was JESUS. †§‡§§

00-20 [_] Do you Understand how Contradictory you are? If the "Word of God" is only ONE Word, who is JESUS, according to the Gospel of John, then Moses must have been Sinning, himself: beCause he Added many Words to the "Word," including the first 5 Books of the "Holy" Bible, which are Self-contradictory, beginning in Chapter 1 of *Genesis,* which is about as Clear as MUD! Otherwise, there might not be 400 Major Religions and 10,000 Sects among each one of them. †§‡§§

00-21 [_] I do not Care whether or not the Bible is Clear and Understandable, just as long as it makes Good Sense to an Ostrich, who has her Head Buried in the Sand. †§‡§§

00-22 [_] You must be a Self-contradictory Medical Doctor, huh?

00-23 [_] I will Murder anyone who does not Believe in the same God that I Believe in. §

00-24 [_] And to which one of the Gods in *Genesis 1:26* are you Referring to?

00-25 [_] How in Hell would I know? I just Believe in GOD; and there is only ONE God, who is ALLAH! †§‡

00-26 [_] Is it any Wonder WHY some of you Muslims are Murdering Innocent People, who do not know their Right Hands from their Left Hands? Why not bring that Unholy Mutilated Bible and the far-less-holy Koran into a Worldwide TELEVISED Courtroom, and Prove them to be True or False, since the Apostle Paul wrote: *"Prove all Provable Things, and Cling Tightly to ALL that is GOOD." — First Thessalonians 5:21,* which seems Reasonable to me? Indeed, are you such a Spiritual COWARD that you cannot Agree to Prove it to be one Way or the other way, and thus Change your Mind, and Conform to whatever Truths are Proven? †‡

00-27 [_] She has been Baptized by some Holy or Unholy GHOST, which is not Willing to Prove anything, much less the Self-contradictory *Bible* and the Insane *Koran*. Moreover, she will likely Deny every Provable Truth within this Inspired Book, whereby she will Remain in the Darkness of Ignorance, FOREVER! †§‡ {See: "The New **MAGNIFIED** Version of the **HOLY KORAN!**" (WHY **MuhamMAD** went to Hell for Spiritual **MURDER!**) By The **Worldwide People's Revolution!®** Book 089.}

00-28 [_] Well, that seems to be very Sad: beCause this Inspired Book Reveals HOW to be Healed from almost all Sicknesses and Diseases, Free of Charge! Guaranteed! ‡

00-29 [_] Well, I was about to Trash this Book; but, after Learning that Information, I do Believe that it will be Wise of me to Study it Carefully. After all, even Huck Finn has no Need for Suffering; but, I suppose that Nigger Jim does: beCause he is Black, while Huck Finn and Tom Sawyer are White, and Chosen Seeds, you might say. †§‡

00-30 [_] Well, many People, who seem to be First in Importance during this Life, may be the Last in Importance during the next Life: beCause of being Born Black: beCause the Gods Control the Destinies of all Spirits of Peoples on and in all Earths. Therefore, White People can be Born in Black Bodies the next Time Around, and Vice Versa, or Wee-kaa Weir-su in Classical Latin. †‡ (See *John 3:27;* and *Matthew 11:14.*) In the Meantime, please tell us WHO Sliced Off that Hardened Steel Column at the World Trade Center (WTC) Towers, during September 11th, 2001?

(Ask Huck Finn and/or Nigger Jim: because neither Tom Sawyer nor Judge Thatcher would Know!)

The Controversial Menu for a Feast of Satisfying Truths!

This Book contains about 50,254 words, and a few Photographs.

— Chapter 01 —

Many who are First shall be Last!

01-01 [_] So, many People who are the First to Learn the Truth, will be the Last to Accept it, huh? But, why is that?

01-02 [_] Well, that is beCAUSE the Gods are only Interested in Obtaining a FEW Good Honest MEN to Govern with them in their Holy Kingdom with their Chosen Sons, one of whom we call "Jesus Christ," who is otherwise known as *The Anointed Savior of this World,"* who came to Save us from all of our Sins, including our Dietary Sins, and to set us Free from all Addictions, Sufferings, Self-inflicted Torments, Pains, Troubles, Wars, Taxes, Debts, Fears, Worries and Woes. Yes, it is now Possible for us to Overcome all of our Sins, and STOP Sinning; but, only IF we Learn the Whole Truth: beCause only the WHOLE Truth can Liberate us from the Prisons of Lies, which we are all Born and Raised in, to some Degree. After all, how else could it be? †§‡

01-03 [_] So, does each one of Countless Worlds have its own Anointed Savior and Supreme Ruler?

01-04 [_] Absolutely — there is no Way around it.

01-05 [_] So, of what Interest are other Worlds to us? Should we be Interested in Learning anything about other Worlds?

01-06 [_] Well, if we are Qualified, we might become the Supreme Rulers of our own Worlds; but, before we can become Qualified, we have to Pass our Tests of Faith, Hope, Trust, Love, Patience, Persistence, and OBEDIENCE to the Laws of the Gods, whose Holy Angels are Keeping Records. †‡

01-07 [_] So, what does any of that have to do with whether or not God or Satan Ordained Medical Doctors? I Fail to Understand the Connection.

01-08 [_] Well, most People would Check that Box with a Green-X, like this [X]: beCause they Agree with you.

01-09 [_] Do you Actually Believe that GOD has anything to do with what is Happening in this World of Woes?

01-10 [_] Well, no matter what I might Believe, it will not Change the Facts by even 2 Degrees. However, it is my Sincere Belief that God has Allowed SATAN to Govern this World for thousands of Years, including all Governments, Churches, Religions, Medical Doctors, Scientists, Lawyers, Judges, Teachers, Professors, Preachers, Priests, and whomever does not Yield to Provable Truths. Yes, I Believe that we are ALL Deceived to some Degree, and Especially if we Imagine that we are NOT Deceived! Indeed, when someone Imagines that he or she is NOT Deceived, it is Proof that he or she is Extremely Ignorant: beCause the more we Learn, the more we Discover that we have been Deceived about a LOT of Important Subjects, which Normally UPSETS us: beCause no one Wants the Foundations of his nor her Life Pulled Out from under him or her, whereby he or she might Collapse with Total Defeat. Therefore, most People just Ignore anything that Contradicts their own Vain Traditions. However, if they cannot Ignore it, they will Ridicule it, Mock it, or at least Refer to it as something "Extreme," or "Radical," and especially if it does not Fit into Mainstream Beliefs — such as the Realities of more than ONE God, who would otherwise be the God of Massive Confusion, if one should Sincerely Believe the "Holy" *Bible,* or the *Koran,* which is Full of Self-contradictions, Foolishness, Absurd Teachings, and Damnable Doctrines — such as those that are Believed by "Radical" Muslims, who have every "Muslim Right" to Misinterpret anything within it, whereby they can Murder Innocent People, while Imagining that they are Serving Allah, who is the Muslim God, who is even more Contradictory and Confused than the Christian God, who Loved the People of the World so much that he supposedly Inspired one of his Disciples to write: *"Love not the World, neither anything that is in the World: beCause, if any Man Loves the World, even as I have Loved the World, the Love of the Father God is not in him: because God so Loved the People of the World that he gave his only Son to Save Mankind in their Sins, who was Begotten by the Power of the Holy Spirit, who came upon Joseph and Mary as they Slept, and Transferred the Holy Seed from the Loins of Joseph into the Womb of Mary, whereby she Conceived a Holy Child called Zeus, in Greek; or Horus, in Egyptian, being the Son of Isis, whom the Professing Christians called Jesus, in English." — The Double Sarcastic Version of First John 2:15.* †§‡§§

01-11 [_] Is there any Truth in that so-called "Quotation"?

01-12 [_] Well, there are some Provable Truths within it. First of all, it is True that God so Loved the People of the World that he Sacrificed his own Chosen Son to Save us FROM all of our Sins, if we should Believe his Inspired Words of Provable Truths, and OBEY them, whereby we might be Saved for Positions within his Good Government. After all, he cannot Save us IN our Sins, or else he would be Contaminating his Holy Kingdom, or Good Government, with Sinners. †‡ {See www.Amazon.com for: "The CONSTITUTION for the New RIGHTEOUS One-World Government!" (HOW all Peoples can get True Justice, and Celebrate the Great Year of JUBILEE!) By The Worldwide People's Revolution!® Book 016B.}

01-13 [_] I have not been Aware that our Salvation has anything to do with a GOVERNMENT, much less the Government of the GODS, which you call the KINGDOM of God — as if Jesus Christ said anything about such a Kingdom. †§‡ (See *Matthew 13*.)

01-14 [_] Apparently you have never "red" the *New Testament,* huh?

01-15 [_] I do not have to "reed" the *New Testament* to know that Jesus Saved me from all of my Sins when I was *"born again,"* having been filled with the Holy Ghost, just after Praying to God that he would provide me with a New Car, which he did, which Actually Belongs to the Banker, who Loaned to me the necessary Money for Buying that Car, which will never Actually be MY Car, halleluJAH: beCause I will never Own it; but, I will make Car Payments, until I get a New Car within a Year or 2, and then make Payments on it. Likewise, that is HOW I will be Qualified for a Position in the Kingdom of God, which I will not Actually Inherit: beCause I am going to Heaven when I Die. (See *John 3:13* for the Proof.) And then, when Jesus Returns with tens of thousands of his Saints, I will Return with him; but, not to Establish any Holy Kingdom on the Earth: beCause the Kingdom of God is in HEAVEN, which is WHY Jesus Prayed, *"Thy Kingdom come to the Earth, and thy Will be Done on the Earth, even as it is now Done in Heavenly Places."* — The Mockingbird's Version of *Matthew 6:10.* †§‡ {See: "Do People Go to Heaven when they Die?" (The Unbelievable Truth about Life and Death!) **By The Good Pastor of Uncommon Sense!** Book 120.}

01-16 [_] Jesus did not Pray any such Prayer, nor did he ask us to Pray any such Prayer. In Fact, this is what he Prayed, *"Our Fathers who are in Heavenly Places, Hallowed are your Holy Names. May your Kingdom come to this Earth, and your Will be Done on this Earth, even as it is now Done in Heavenly Places: beCause you have Created Countless Worlds to be Inhabited with your Peoples, who come in all Shapes, Sizes, Colors, and Kinds. Yes, please Give to us this Day our Daily Foods: beCause we are far too Lazy to Grow our own Foods. For Example, it might Require all of 10 Minutes to Plant a Fig Tree, which could Grow up to Feed a Person, or even an entire Family, if it is Cared for Properly, which might Require an average of 10 Minutes per Day to Fertilize and Water such a Tree. Therefore, please Forgive us for Borrowing any Money to Buy Foods that we should be Growing, ourselves: beCause it is a Sin to be in Debt to other People. In Fact, O Gods, no one should have to Borrow any Money from anyone: beCause a Righteous GovernMINT would simply Mint and Print the Necessary New Money to Hire us to Build our own Houses, Plant our own Gardens, Make our own Cisterns for Water Storage, and Build our own Terraced Stone Walls, which would Represent that New Money, which would have to be Earned by Honest Labor. Moreover, any Chiild with a Riit Miind could Understand that. Therefore, do not let us Lead ourselves into Foolish Temptations to Borrow Money, when Bankers are not Needed for True Prosperity, even as Medical Doctors are not Needed for Obtaining Good Health, or else the Billions of Wild Animals would have never Obtained it. Therefore, please Deliver us from all such Evils: beCause yours is the Kingdom, the Power, and the Glory Forever. Amen."* — The Enlightening Version. †§‡§§

01-17 [_] I am Totally Discombobulated by all such Prayers. However, I must Confess that the English Grammar is more Accurate than the King James Version, which is a Disaster. ‡

01-18 [_] So, is that True — that Bankers are not Needed for True Prosperity?

01-19 [_] Well, did you Meditate on the Words in that Quote in Verse 01-16? Did it cross your Mind that a few Fruit Trees could actually Feed you, whereby you could Avoid going to some Gross Grocery Store to look for some Unsatisfying Inferior Food Stuffings? ‡

01-20 [_] Well, I would never be Contented to Eat nothing but Figs, even if such a Tree could Feed me. Besides that, it would not be a Balanced Diet, which Requires that all Panda Bears Eat at the Pizza Huts: beCause a Steady Diet of Bamboo Shoots cannot Feed a Panda Bear all that it Needs to Live, which is WHY that I saw a Panda Bear Eating from a Garbage Can: beCause it was Obviously Starving to Death on those Bamboo Shoots, for the Lack of a Well-balanced Diet. And I am NOT being Sarcastic. †§‡§§ (But, you *are* being Sarcastic.)

01-21 [_] So, is it True that John the Baptist Lived on nothing but Wild Honey and Locust Fruits? (See *Matthew 3:4;* and *Mark 1:6.*)

01-22 [_] Well, I have no Cause to Doubt it, do you?

01-23 [_] Would he not have been Deprived of Necessary Foods?

01-24 [_] Such as … ?

01-25 [_] Well, such as Camel's Milk, Rats, Lizards and Snakes. §

01-26 [_] So, if a Well-balanced Diet is not Necessary, why does the *Bible* not List the Horrible Diseases that the Children of Israel Contracted when they Lived on nothing but Manna for 40 Years? †§‡

01-27 [_] The Wording is not Correct. It should say, "If a Well-balanced Diet of Hog Slop and Dog Foods is Necessary, why does the *Bible* not List the Horrible Diseases that the Children of Israel Contracted when they Lived on nothing but Manna for 40 Years?" Indeed, it specifically States that those Children had NO Sicknesses nor Diseases for 40 Years: beCause of Eating nothing but Manna! ‡ (See *Psalm 78.*)

01-28 [_] I do not have a *Bible* to read; and I would not Trust it, even if I did Read it. ‡§

01-29 [_] Well, for your Sake, I will Quote it to you within the next Chapter.

01-30 [_] And will it be the Pure Truth, or just another Perverted Version, like the following very Long Boring Quotation from *Numbers 11,* from Verse A to Z?

> A-[_] And when the People Complained about their Poor Diet, it Displeased the Supreme Ruler: because he Overheard them; and therefore, his Anger was Kindled against them; and the Fire of the Supreme Ruler Burned among them, and Consumed those People who were in the Outermost Parts of the Camp, who were Afraid to get near to his Holy Tabernacle: because, to them, he was an Austere God, who did not Rule them with Love nor Compassion, as one would Expect from a Heavenly Father, who could Relate with the Weaknesses of Mankind. And thus, the People Cried unto Moses, begging him for Meat and Bread: because they Remembered the Flesh Pots and Ovens in Egypt, which filled the Air with the Aroma of Fresh Baked Bread. However, when they saw the Fire of God among them, and how it Consumed the Worst of them, they Cried Out to Moses with

Great Tears in their Eyes, while Begging him to Please Save them. Therefore, when Moses Prayed to Yohoovu God, the Fire was Quenched; and he called the Name of that Place Taberu: because the Fire of Yohoovu had Burned among them.

B-[ ] And it came to pass, later on, that the Mixed Multitude of Colored People who were among them, who were perhaps the most Ignorant of all Peoples on the Earth, fell into Lusting after that Flesh that they Remembered: because they had Longing Desires to Eat it again; and the Children of Israel also Wept again, and said: "Who shall give to us Flesh to Eat? Why do we have to be Deprived of the Good Things in this Life? Yes, we Remember the Fishes, which we Ate in Egypt, freely — even also the Cucumbers, Melons, Leeks, Onions, Garlic, and Various Kinds of Spices; but, now our Souls are all Dried up, and our Flesh has Withered Away: because there is nothing at all to Eat, except for this Hateful Boring Manna, which is Detestable in our Eyes." And the Manna was like Coriander Seeds is Size and Shape, and the Color thereof was Bdellium, which was like Mouse Turds in Appearance; but, it Tasted like Burro Butter that is Mixed with Wild Honey, which was actually quite Pleasant and Satisfying. Moreover, the People went all about with their Baskets, and Gathered it up, and Ground it in Stone Mills, which they had brought from Egypt: because there was not a Proper Stone anywhere near Mount Sinai, which might be used for making such Mills, which they knew Instinctively before they Departed from Egypt. Otherwise, they Beat the Manna with Pestles and Mortars, which they had also brought with them from Egypt; and thus they Baked it in Pans, in Ovens, which Pans they had also brought with them from Egypt, along with any Firewood: because there were no Trees in that Great Desert, whereby 6 Million People could have Warmed themselves with Fires for more than a Day or 2; and thus, they made Manna Cakes of it, and the Taste of it was as Good as anything that People had ever Eaten since the Time of Adam, being Sweeter than Fresh Oil from Nuts. And when the Dew fell on the Camp during the Night, the Manna fell with it: because it Rained Down from Heaven — that is, from the Sky, and not from Orion, nor from any Distant Earth; but, from the Clouds in the Sky. †§‡

C-[ ] Then Moses Heard the Peoples Weeping throughout their Families, every Man in the Doorway of his Tent, being like

Spoiled Babies, whose Hearts were Set on Vain Things that they did not Need for their True Happiness, which comes from having Good Health and True Love. Nevertheless, Moses did not Condemn them for it: because he was also getting Tired of Eating that Boring Manna. Nevertheless, the Anger of Yohoovu was Greatly Kindled, like a very Hot Fire; and Moses was also Displeased with them: because of their Murmurings: because he knew that they would never be Satisfied, no matter what they might have, nor how much of it that they might have: because that is the Nature of Lusts, which can never be Satisfied. And therefore, Moses said to Yohoovu, "Why have you Afflicted your Servants with this Boring Manna? And why have I found Favor in your Sight, so that you lay the Burdens of all of these Peoples on me? Did I Conceive all of these Peoples? Have I Begotten them, so that you should say to me: 'Carry them in your Bosom,' even as a Nursing Father Bears the Sucking Child for his Mother, unto the Land that you Swore to Give unto their Fathers? Why do you not Transform this Worthless Desert into a Better Promised Land, and make it a Good Place for them to Live? After all, no one has ever Lived here, nor could anyone care less who does Live here. From where shall I have Flesh to Give to all of these Hungry People, whose Bones protrude like those of Old Cattle? Yes, they Weep in my Ears, saying: 'Give to us Flesh to Eat, so that we might be Satisfied.' I am not able to Bear all of these Peoples, alone: because they are too Heavy for me to Carry. Therefore, if you must Deal thus with me, why do you not just Kill me by some Accident, if I have found Favor in your Sight, whereby I might Rest myself a little; and let me not see my own Wretchedness: because I too am just Skin and Bones, you might say. Yes, even a Wild Ass has more Flesh on his Bones than I have." †

D-[ ] And Yohoovu said to Moses, "Gather unto me Seventy-two Men from among the Elders of Israel, whom you know to be the Elders of my Chosen People, and Officers over them; and bring them unto the Tabernacle of the Congregation, so that they might Stand there with you; but, do not bring the Colored Peoples with you: beCause they are altogether Unclean and Uncivilized, being far too Ignorant to Inherit any Positions within my Holy Kingdom. Nevertheless, if they Sincerely Repent, and Purify themselves, their Spirits may be Born into your Families, and thus be Adopted into my Chosen Family, who have Blond Hairs and Blue Eyes, even as the Holy Angels have: beCause it is Symbolical of Purity, even as the Blue Flames of a very Hot Fire. Yes, Black is Symbolical of Uncleanness, while White is Symbolical of Purity. However, there will come a Time when Black People will be more Honest and Pure in their Hearts than the White People, who will become Liars, Deceivers, and Greedy Money-mongers and Warmongers: beCause their Hearts will not be Right with their Great Creator God, as they should be. Indeed, they will become all Puffed Up with Great Pride, as if they Created themselves; but, behold, Pride comes before Destruction, and a Haughty Spirit before a Fall. Therefore, it is not Good for them to Build Up their Pride, whereby I will have to Humble them, and Cause their Spirits to be Born in Black Bodies, whereby they will be made into Slaves, and thus, be Humiliated for it, until they Confess the Truths that I Teach, and thus, Change their Ways of Thinking and Living. And I will come down and Talk with you from the Tabernacle, from the Most Holy Place; and I will take of the Spirit that is upon you, and will put it upon those Elders; and they will Bear the Burdens of the Peoples with you, so that you do not Bear all such Burdens by yourself, alone: because I See that it is too much for you; and I am Sorry that I did not See it sooner. Yes, you should have told me about it a long Time Ago, if it was too much for you: beCause I cannot Reed Minds, as you might Think — at least not normally, or else I might Foresee what is Needed among your Peoples. After all, I have never Lived in a Human Body. Therefore, you must Try to Understand where I am coming from: beCause I can hardly Relate with you. Moreover, say to the Peoples, 'Sanctify yourselves against Tomorrow, and get Prepared to Eat Flesh: because you have Wept in the Ears of the Supreme Ruler, saying: "Who shall Give to us Flesh to Eat — for it was Well with us in Egypt, when we could Fill our Stomachs with Fishes and all Kinds of Good-tasting Things?" But, it was not Well.' Therefore, tell them no more than that: because the Supreme Ruler will Give to them Flesh, and they shall Eat all that they Lust after. However, they shall not Eat it for just one Day, nor for 2 Days, nor for 5 Days, neither 10 nor 20 Days; but, even a whole Month of 28 Days, until it is Running Out of their Nostrils in the Form of Snot and Slime: because they shall Catch Colds. Yes, it will Fill their Heads with Mucus and Slime, whereby they will hardly be able to Breathe; and therefore, it will become Loathsome to them: beCause they have Despised the Supreme Ruler, who is among them, who has not been

Eating anything, and they have Wept in front of him, saying: 'Why did we come forth Out of Egypt, when it would have been Better for us to have Stayed in Egypt, where we could have at least Eaten Well?' Therefore, they shall get the Desires of their own Hearts, and Learn their Lessons the most Difficult Way Possible with Sicknesses and Diseases, when they could have just Trusted my Words of Provable Truths, and Obeyed them." And thus, Moses was Astonished that God could not Read Minds. †§‡

E-[_] And Moses said, "The People, among whom I am, are 600,000 Footmen ready for War, besides their Families, their Wives, their Babies, their Children, and their Old Folks; yes, there are Millions of them, and yet you have said, 'I will Give to them Flesh to Eat, so that they might Eat it for a whole Month of 28 Days.' Shall the Flocks of Sheeps and Goats and the Herds of Cattles be Slain for them to Eat, just to Suffice their Lusts? Or, shall all of the Fishes of the Sea be Gathered Together to Feed them, just to Satisfy their Endless Cravings, not to mention those of the millions of Heathen Peoples among us, who wanted to get Out of the Bondage in Egypt, who came along with us?"

F-[_] And Yohoovu God said to Moses, "Has the Hand of the Supreme Ruler Grown Short, so that it cannot Reach unto the Ends of the Earth? You shall See now whether or not my Words shall come to pass: beCause I will Cause the Angels of the Winds to Obey my Voice, and they will Sweep Up Quails for you to Eat, and not just a few of them. Indeed, they will Fill the Sky and Darken the Sunlight with their Multitudes."

G-[_] And Moses went out, and told the People all of the Words of the Supreme Ruler, which he had Commanded him, and Gathered the Seventy-two Men from among the Elders of the People of Israel, and set them around the Tabernacle in 12 little Bands, having 6 in each Band from all 12 Tribes, so that they could not Complain about any Injustices for not having Representatives to Represent each Tribe, Equally and Justly, whereby each Man's Vote would Count on behalf of his Tribe when making any Decisions: beCause it was a Representative Government of each Tribe, which Selected those Elders from among them, and Sent them to Moses. And thus, the Supreme Ruler came down in a Cloud, and Spoke to Moses, and took a Portion of the Spirit that was upon him, and Gave it to the

Seventy-two Elders; and it came to pass, that when the Spirit Rested on them, they were Filled with the Holy Spirit, and they threw off all of their Clothing and Prophesied, and did not Cease until Sunset. However, there remained 2 of the Men in the Camp, whose Names were Eldad and Meedad, who went on Prophesying, who were Written among the Number of them who had been Elected; but, they did not go Out of the Camp nor Into the Tabernacle; but, they Prophesied in the Camp, even among those Black and Mixed Colors of Races, who soon took up a Chant, whereby they Sang the same Song, over and over and OVER, until they went into a Frenzy, and Lost Control of their Minds, and Cast Off all of their Clothing, also, as if they had been Filled with the Holy Spirit; but, Satan had Deceived them: beCause he has an Imitation and Counterfeit Spirit for every Spirit of the Gods; but, not for Good, as some People might Imagine; but, for Deceptions and Lies: beCause that is his Calling and Occupation, in Order for God to Test the Spirits of Mankind. Nevertheless, a Young Man ran and told Moses about it, saying: "Moses! Moses! Eldad and Meedad are Prophesying in the Camp among the Black People, who have Cast Off all of their Clothing, and are Rolling around Naked on the Ground, and Speaking in Strange Unknown Languages, as if they have gone Mad! Therefore, what shall we Do with them?" †§‡

H-[_] And Joshua, the Son of Nun, even the Servant of Moses, and one of his most Trusted Young Men, Answered him, saying: "Call the Elders Together for a Meeting of the Minds: beCause Moses is Tired of his Burdens with these Peoples." But, while the Young Man was Calling the Elders, Joshua said to Moses, "My Ruler Moses, should we not Forbid Eldad and Meedad from Prophesying?" †‡

I-[_] And Moses Answered him, "Do you Envy them for my Sake? I wish to God that all of Yohoovu's People were Prophets, and that the Supreme Ruler would put his Spirit upon all of them! However, I See that Satan has come among those Black People, who Chanted themselves into a Frenzied State of Mind, whereby Evil Spirits now have Control Over them, even as they will have during the Last Days, before the Second Coming of the Messiah, when they will Vainly Imagine that they are Speaking in other Languages, when it will be nothing but Gibberish and Nonsense: beCause that is what Chanting does to Weak Minds. Therefore, be sure to Write it in the Books of Remembrance, so as to Warn the True Sons of Jacob about all such Evils, so that they do not Fall Headlong into any such Deep Dark Pits." And Joshua got Moses into the Camp with the Elders, once again. †‡

J-[_] And there went forth a Mighty Wind from the Supreme Ruler, and it brought in Quails from the Sea, as if the Fishes had been Transformed into Quails; and the Wind let them Fall by the Camp, as it were a Day's Journey on all Sides of it, all around the Encampment of the Israelites and the Mixed Multitudes of the Nations, who numbered in the tens of Millions, who had Migrated from Africa: beCause of a Great Famine, who Heard that there was Manna in the Wilderness of Arabia, even in the Desert, where nothing but Lizards and Snakes could Live, you might say. Moreover, the Quails were 2 feet Deep, all around the Camp: beCause of the Great Flocks of Birds that the Angels of the Winds had brought upon them. Yes, there were not only Quails; but, there were Pheasants, Chickens, Turkeys, Guinea Fowls, Ducks, Geese, and many Kinds of Birds. And thus, the People stood up all that Day, and all that Night, and all of the next Day, Gathering the Quails and other Birds, to Undress them and Gut them, and Prepare them to Eat. Yes, they Salted many of them, in order to Cure them and Smoke them, so as to Eat them later on. Indeed, he who Gathered the Least Amount Gathered no less than 50 Bushels of them, and Stacked them in Piles all around the Camp, and Cooked many of them in Pots, and Baked many of them in Ovens that they Constructed in the Ground with Hot Rocks under and around and on top of them, whereby they could Feast on them. And they did Feast on them, all Night and all Day, even for 28 whole Days they Glutted themselves on those Birds, as if Starved half to Death; but, the 72 Elders and Moses did not Eat with them; but, they Fasted and Prayed for them. And while the Flesh was still between their Teeth, before it was thoroughly Chewed on the 28th Day, the Wrath of the Supreme Ruler was Kindled against the Mixed Multitude, and also against the Children of Israel, who Partook of their Sins; and thus, the Supreme Ruler Smote the Peoples with a very Great Plague, and Slew the Fattest of them. And he called the Name of that Place Kibrothhattaauvu: beCause there they Buried the People who had Lusted after Flesh to Eat; but, none of their Bones have ever been Discovered. However, even if they were Discovered, they would not be Israelite Bones: beCause they were the Bones of the Mixed Multitude. And the People Journeyed from Kibrothhattaauvu unto Hazeroth, along the Red Sea; and they Lived there in Tents, and Fasted and Prayed for Mercy: beCause the Austere God was not Finished with them. No, not by any Means: beCause he was Determined to bring them to Perfection for either Good or Evil, at whatever the Costs. †§‡

K-|_| Now, it came to pass that after much Fasting and Praying, Moses, Aaron, Hur, Joshua and the 72 Elders had another Great Meeting of the Most-Intelligent Minds at Hazeroth, and Moses said: "Thank God that we still have Manna to Eat. Indeed, I was Worried that Yohoovu God might Stop it from coming down, and just let us Die in this Wilderness; but, I See that he is Determined to bring us to Perfection for either Good or Evil, and at whatever the Costs: beCause he has Revealed to me that he has been Dealing with our Souls for Millions of Years, and is getting Tired of our Rebellions. Nevertheless, he has also Revealed to me that it will Require several thousands of more Years of Torments to bring us to Perfection: beCause we are so Slow to Learn our Lessons. Therefore, it shall come to pass during the Last Days, before the Establishment of a New Righteous One-World Government, that the Masses of People will be in Great Distress, and in a Great Tribulation, being Tormented on all Sides, you might say, while being very Perplexed by the Situations, who will seem to have no Remedy for anything. Nevertheless, the Supreme Ruler will raise up a Special King, who will Set the House in Order, you might say, who will Act Wisely and Discreetly, so as to make himself Popular among the Masses of People, who will Cheerfully Elect him to be their Righteous King: beCause he will Promise to make almost all of them Moderately Rich, just by their Labors, alone, whose Good Government will have 6 High Priests from 6 Major Religions, 60 Elected Kings from 60 Major Nations, and a Maximum of 600 Elected Governors from Minor Nations and from the Islands of the Seas: beCause he will have a Small, Efficient and Effective Good Government: beCause he will Inspire the Masses of People to Build Beautiful Planned City States for themselves, whereby each City State will Govern itself, according to its own Elected Laws and Flexible Rules, whereby all of the Peoples can be Happy: beCause, if someone does not Love one certain City, such a Person may Move to another City State with more Likable People. After all, not everyone Thinks just Alike. Therefore, the Masses of People will get to Choose whatever they Like, and Willingly Experiment with Different Diets, According to their Lusts and Longing Desires, while other People will Choose to be Ascetics: beCause of Wanting to become like the Gods, themselves, who are Pure in all Ways. Therefore, it will be the Most-Interesting Time to Live, in the History of Mankind: beCause the Furnace of Afflictions will become very HOT, just before that Great King is Elected, whereby People will Suffer with all Kinds of Sicknesses and Diseases, and will Waste much Money on Witchdoctors, Lawyers, Divorces, Wars, and many Vain Things — such as their Horseless Chariots and Wagons, which many People will Worship, in spite of getting Killed by them, even as they will also Worship those Witchdoctors, in spite of Wasting much Money on them, and in spite of Suffering more Deaths by them, than by Wars: beCause of not Learning their Lessons from what we Experienced in Kibrothhattaauvu, where we Buried the Peoples who Lusted after Flesh, which was in Deed Running Out of their Nostrils, just as God had Predicted it to me, alone, which any Doctor with even half of his Brains could Prove for himself, if he Experimented Scientifically with it. Yes, he could Feast on some Flesh of whatever Kind he Loves for himself, until it Runs Out of his Nose, and thus, Discover the Source of his Sickness or Disease, as a Result of Eating too much Flesh, which is also True of Cheese, Butter, Milk, Eggs, Bread, and many other Slimy Sticky Foods, and Especially Sugar and Greasy Foods: beCause the Grease will Stick in the Bowels, just like it Sticks in your Frying Pans, whereby it must be Washed Out with Hot Water, Soap and a Scrub Brush: beCause it is very Sticky Stuff. However, no one Scrubs Out their Bowels with any such Hot Water, Soap, nor anything else: beCause that is an Impossibility. However, it is not Impossible to Eat Sweet Fruits, which will Help to Dissolve all such Sticky Stuff, along with Pure Water. Yes, Lemons and Limes are Good for that, except that the Acids in them can also Dissolve your Precious Teeth. Therefore, you have to Know what you are Doing, in Order to not Damage yourself. Indeed, many Egyptians made Bad Decisions, Years Ago, whereby they Learned how to Fast and Eat Properly to some Degree, which is why none of them were Fat, if you Recall. Nevertheless, we do not have Fresh Sweet Fruits to Eat in this Wilderness of Sins: beCause they do not Grow here. However, they will Grow Well in the Promised Land, and then you may Feast on them." †§‡

L-[_] And Joshua, being Young and Bright-minded, said: "But, how Long will it be before we get to the Promised Land?"

M-|_| And Moses Answered, "Well, to tell you the Truth, you will have to be Born in it: beCause it is on the Inside of the Hollow Earth. However, only the Most Righteous Souls will be Born there: beCause this Outside World was Prepared for those Souls who are Slow to Learn their Lessons, who have to Suffer with Various Kinds of Evils, just to come to their Right Senses. Therefore, do not Think any Evil Thoughts, nor Do any Evil Works; and then you may be Born there, even in the Holy City of the Great King, if you are Found Worthy of it, which is also in the Hollow Earth." †‡

N-[_] And Joshua said, "And do you Expect the Normal Person to Believe all of that? Moreover, how can we go into the Promised Land that Father Abraham Inherited, and Kill all of the Inhabitants thereof, without Thinking any Evil Thoughts?" †‡

O-|_| And Moses Answered him, "I do not Expect the Normal Person to Believe any of those Words; but, that is Okay: beCause the Normal Person does not have the Slightest Chance of Entering Into the Holy Kingdom of All that is GOOD: beCause only the Ascetics will Stand a Chance of it: beCause of Self-discipline. Nevertheless, that does not Mean that all other Souls will be Lost, nor Condemned to some Fiery Hell, as you might Imagine: beCause they will be Saved for Servants of the Righteous Ones, if only they Confess their Faith in the Anointed Savior, who will Save them from their Sins, whereby they may Qualify to Continue to Live in this World of Wonders. Otherwise, their Spirits will be Cast Down to a Lower Order of Worlds, where they will be Tormented Seven Times more than here! Yes, God has Revealed to me that there are Countless Worlds, which must be Inhabited by Peoples, who will have to be Refined and Purified to some Degree, just to be Found Worthy to Live here, at all; but, to Live in Mount Zion, they will have to become HOLY, even as the Anointed Savior is Holy. Therefore, everyone who has that Hope within himself, Purifies himself, even as he is Pure. However, to Answer your Question about not Thinking Evil Thoughts, while Murdering the Canaanites, Hittites, Hiivites, Perizites, Jebuzites, and the other Ites in the Promised Land, just Remember that you will be doing a Great Service for them: beCause you will be Freeing their Spirits for New Bodies, who may be Born in Israelite Families, where you can Teach to them these Great Truths. Moreover, beCause of Murdering them, you will also have to be Born in Heathen Families, where you can be Tested for your Faith in my Inspired Words of Provable Truths. Yes, you have no Idea WHERE nor WHEN you will be Born here nor there; but, you can be Sure that if you Think Evil Thoughts, or Do any Evil Deeds, you will not Inherit a Good Place to Live; while the Righteous Person will Inherit such a Place, and will be most Thankful for it." †§‡

P-[_] And Joshua said, "So, it Sounds as if we are Trapped between a Rock and a Stone Wall, huh? No matter which Way we go, we are Doomed to X-amount of Suffering, huh? Is that not something like Predestination?" †§‡

Q-[_] And Moses Answered, "The Great Question is this, '**Will we be Perfected during this Life, or during the next Life??**' Well, if we are Predestined to Live this Way or that Way, then we could not Change it, could we? Therefore, if we cannot Change it, how can God Condemn us for it during the Day of Judgment? Indeed, he cannot Rightly Condemn us, no matter what we Say nor Do: beCause we are Predestined to Say and Do those Things. Therefore, that is HOW the Gods will Save almost all of us: beCause we will be Saved on Account of our IGNORANCE; but, we will NOT be Saved for Positions within the Holy Kingdom of the Gods: beCause that Requires that we Willingly CHOOSE to Do what is RIGHT for ourselves and others; and it is NOT Right to Murder Innocent People, even if they are as Black as Coal, nor as White as Snow: beCause Murder is Murder, no matter how you go about Doing it; and the Punishment for it is DEATH: beCause, he who Sheds Man's Blood, so shall his Blood be Shed, and Endlessly so, until People Wake Up and Come to their Right Senses, and Thoroughly REPENT. Yes, that is the KEY to the Kingdom, you might say, which Requires HOLINESS of Mind, Spirit, and Body, which cannot be Obtained while Feasting with the Dogs nor Hogs." †‡

R-[_] And Joshua said, "So, in the Resurrection, will we be Justified for Murdering those Poor Ignorant Canaanites, whose Spirits may be Born in Israelite Families?" †

S-[_] And Moses Answered him, "Satan would have you to Believe that Lie; but, the Holy Spirit of the Gods tells me that only Innocent People will Enter into the Holy Kingdom. Therefore, if you Murder any such Souls, you must Understand that you are also Consigning your own Spirit to a Black Person's Body: beCause that is the Punishment for Doing it, whether or not you are Black or White." †‡

T-[_] Therefore, Joshua said, "So, why does Yohoovu God Demand and Command us to Kill those Canaanites, Knowing that we will be Consigning our Spirits to be Born in Black Bodies for the Punishment that we Deserve for Doing it? Indeed, if God Knows that, why does he not Kill them, himself, by Means of some Plague, Poison, Disease, Fever, Tornado, Earthquake, Volcano, or some other Natural Disaster?" †‡

U-[_] And Moses Answered, "Well, you must Understand that God could do that for you; but, in this Case, God is Testing your Obedience to his Commandments, which he would not otherwise ever Do: beCause he Hates Murders. However, by Murdering those Canaanites, you will be Liberating your own Souls: beCause of Obeying that Strange Commandment of God, which seems to be Unjust." †‡

V-[_] And Joshua said, "So, if we Murder the Canaanites, we will get the Victory over them, and God will Forgive us for it: beCause of Obeying his Voice, huh?" †‡

W-[_] And Moses Answered, "Well, I would certainly Hate to have to Prove that in a Courtroom: beCause it makes no Sense to a Weak Mind like mine. Perhaps Yohoovu God has gone Insane?" †§‡

X-[_] And Aaron Spoke up, saying: "X-number of People will Misunderstand the Commandments of God, and even Imagine that they are also Doing some Special Service for God by Murdering Innocent People during the Future, whereby they will bring Double Damnation onto themselves!" †‡

Y-[_] And Hur Spoke up, saying: "Yesterday I had Great Peace of Mind; but, Today, I am Greatly Confused, and have no Idea what to Think — except that this Religious Nonsense is enough to Drive a Person INSANE! How can we Do Good by Doing Evils?" †§‡

Z-[_] And the Most-High God said, "I did not Ask you to Do any Evil. Indeed, that was Satan who Spoke to you in my Name: beCause he is a Great Deceiver, who cannot be Trusted. Therefore, you have Hopefully Learned a Good Lesson from him. Yes, if anyone Asks you to Say or Do any Evil Thing, it is a Thing from Satan, the Devil: beCause he is the Father and Inventor of all Evils, including the Murdering of Canaanites, Hittites, Hiivites, Jebuzites, and any other Ites. Indeed, the Right Way to Solve all such Problems in a Peaceful Manner, is to Call for a Great Meeting of the Most-Intelligent Minds, whereby you Resolve your Problems with Reasonable Solutions. For Example, this Desert can be made into a Habitable Place, if you Think about it; and then you will not have to go into any so-called *'Promised Land,'* and thus make Murderers of yourselves. Nevertheless, in order to make this Land Habitable, you will have to figure out how to Transform that Salty Sea Water into Fresh Water: beCause you cannot Grow any Crops without it. However, I will Feed you with Manna, until you get your Planned Cities Built. Moreover, you will also have to Discover some Mountains of Good Rocks to Work with, so as to Build Beautiful Planned City States in this Desert. Therefore, you will need the Assistance of other Nations, whom you may also Help to Build their own Beautiful Planned City States, whereby you can Overcome all Evils by Doing GOOD, which is According to my Master Plan, without the Shedding of any Innocent Blood." †§‡

— Chapter 02 —

The New MAGNIFIED Version of PSALM 78 in Plain English!

02-01 [_] Open your Spiritual Ears, and Listen to my Inspired Words of Provable Truths, O my People, and Understand my Laws; yes, incline your Ears to Hear the Words of my Mouth: beCause they are not in Vain, nor Insane. Indeed, I will open my Mouth and Speak in a Parable: beCause Parables are very Good for Learning Lessons. Therefore, I will Utter Dark and Mysterious Sayings of Ancient Times, which we have Heard and Known to be True, and our Fathers have also told the same Great Truths in many Ways.

02-02 [_] Therefore, we will not Hide the Truth about the Human Body and Mind, nor Cover it up with Blankets; but, we will Uncover it, and Show it in Plain View to whomever has Eyes to See, while Showing to the Generation to come the Praises of the Great Creator God, who Designed every Body to Heal itself, without the Use of any Drugs, nor Medicines, or else the Great Creator God would have been a God of Injustices: beCause he did not provide Hands for the Wild Animals, whereby they might Earn Money, whereby they might Buy some Drugs, which are Sold by Witchdoctors. Behold, the Strength of the Supreme Ruler is Immeasurable, and his Wonderful Works that he has done are most Marvelous, which anyone can Study, even of the Human Body, and thus Discover how Marvelous our Bodies and Minds are. However, some Foolish People Refuse to even Look into your Eyes, which are the Windows of your Soul.

02-03 [_] Nevertheless, Yohoovu God Established a Testimony in the Mouth of Jacob, and Appointed Divine Laws among the Children of Israel, which he Commanded our Fathers, so that they should make those Laws known to their Children: so that the Generation to come might Learn them, even the Children that shall be Born, who should Arise from the Dead when they are Born Again: because all Spirits are Recycled, again and again; and thus they can Declare those Commandments to their Children: so that they can set their Hope in Yohoovu God, and not Forget the Great Works of the Holy Gods when they Look up at the Multitude of Stars during the Darkness of Night; but, Remember to Keep and Obey their Commandments: so that they might not be like their Foolish Forefathers, who were of a Stubborn and Rebellious Generation — even a Generation that did not set their Hearts Aright, and whose Spirits were not Steadfast with the Gods, who are as One: beCause they are in Perfect Agreement concerning Basic Truths. Moreover, we should become One with them, and also be in Perfect Agreement, which is our Destiny, if we have Good Spirits. Otherwise, we will be Adopted into the Family of Satan, and become Demons.

02-04 [_] Indeed, the Children of Ephraim, being Armed with Weapons, and Carrying Bows and Arrows, turned back during the Day of Battle. They did not Keep the Covenant of Yohoovu God, and Refused to Live According to his Laws; and also Forgot about his Works, and his Great Wonders that he had Shown to them in Egypt. Yes, he did Marvelous Things in the Sight of their Fathers, in the Land of Egypt, in the Fields of Zoan, which Moses forgot to write about with Details: because he Judged that the Instructions for the Tabernacle were more Important in his Books. Nevertheless, he went on to Divide the Red Sea, whereby part of it went to the North, and a part to the South, and Caused the Children of Israel to pass through the Bottom of the Red Sea on Dry Ground, while he made the Waters to Stand Up as a Heap on both Sides of them by Strong Fierce Winds, which Blew the Waters back by 10 Miles on each Side of them, and Held them there, while the Children of Faith passed across the Bottom of the Red Sea during 3 Months: because there were about 6 Million of them, along with Great Herds of Livestocks, with Cattles, Camels, Horses, Mules, Sheeps, Goats, and with Flocks of Chickens, Turkeys, and other Birds: because they had Spoiled the Egyptians, and had taken their Wagons, and Loaded them with Silver and Gold and Cooking Utensils and Furniture and Clothing and Precious Things. Therefore, it Required a long Time for them to Move through the 200-mile-wide and one-quarter-mile-deep Bottom of the Hot and Miserable Red Sea with so many Creatures, who had to be let down by Ropes over the many Cliffs in the Sea; and then be Raised Up by Ropes on the other Side: because of the Steep Cliffs, which are about 200 Meters High, altogether: because it is the Nature of the Red Sea. Moreover, they had to Pack all of their Foods and Drinking Water with them during those Months: because the Salty Sea Water was not fit to Drink. However, they Dug Wells in the Bottom of the Sea, in order to Obtain Fresh Water as they went along: because there was Groundwater, and plenty of it. After all, the Livestock could have easily Drank 100 million Gallons of Water per Day! †§‡

02-05 [_] Yohoovu God also Led them during the Daytime by Means of a Cloud, in order to Shade them from the Horrible Heat in that Great Wilderness, while he Led them all Night with a Pillar of Fire, whereby he Warmed them: because it is Freezing Cold in that Desert at Night, whereby your Teeth would be Clacking without it or some other Fire, or at least some Heavy Woolen Blankets. †§‡

02-06 [_] He Split the Rocks in the Wilderness, and gave to them Drinks of Sweet Coconut Water, even as Abundant as the Water from the Great Depths of the Red Sea. Yes, he brought Streams of Water out of the Rocks, and Caused Waters to run down like Rivers all about them: because such a Great Multitude could easily Drink up a River of Water every Day. †§‡

02-07 [_] And yet they Sinned more against Yohoovu God by Provoking the Most-High God in the Wilderness, whereby they Tempted the Gods to Destroy them: because of Lusting after Flesh to Eat: because their Hearts were still in Egypt, you might say, and their Minds were dwelling on Recipes of Dainty Dishes of Forbidden Foods. Yes, they spoke against God, saying: "Can God furnish a Table in the Wilderness? Behold, he Split the Rocks, so that Waters gushed out of them, and the Streams overflowed with fresh Coconut Water for both Man and Beast to Drink; but, can he give to us Bread and Butter to Eat with Sweet Honey? Can he provide Sweet Spicy Flesh for his People to Eat?" †§‡

02-08 [_] Therefore, Yohoovu Heard that Chatter, and was very Angry with it, whereby an Evil Fire was Kindled against the Sons of Jacob, and Fierce Anger also came up against the Dawterz of Israel, who Inspired their Husbands to Murmur and Complain, who might otherwise have been Contented: because they Believed in God, and Trusted in his Salvation; but, those Dawterz did not Believe in God, nor Trust in his Salvation, even though he had Commanded the Clouds from above, and had Opened the Doors and Windows of Heaven, and had Rained down Manna upon them to Eat, and had given to them of the Bread of Heaven. Yes, Mankind Ate Angels' Food, and they Satisfied their Hunger with those Sweet and Oily Grains, which were Better than anything that had Grown in Egypt. †‡

02-09 [_] Nevertheless, the Children of Israel persisted with their Complaints for Flesh to Eat. Therefore, Yohoovu God caused an East Wind to Blow in the Sky, whereby he sent Meat to them, until they were Full of it, even until the Slime was Running Out of their Nostrils, just as it is written in *the Book of Numbers, Chapter 11;* and by his Mighty Power he brought in the South Wind, and Rained Flesh upon them like Dust, and Feathered Fowls like the Sand of the Sea; and he let it fall in the midst of their Camp, and all around about their Habitations, which stretched out for hundreds of Miles: because one can hardly find a flat place in all of that Wilderness to even Pitch a Tent: because it is Covered with Rough Rocks and Rocky Mountains, being one of the most Miserable Places on the entire Earth to Live, which is why no one Livz there. Nevertheless, they Ate Flesh and were Filled with it: because God gave to them whatever they Craved for; and they were not Withheld from their Lusts: because they needed to Learn Hard Lessons, which they could have Learned from Reading Good Books: because History often Rhymes with itself. Therefore, while the Flesh was still in their Mouths, the Wrath of God came upon them, and Slew the Fattest of them, and Killed the Chosen Men of Israel, even those who had Escaped from Egypt by Miracles and Great Wonders. †§‡

02-10 [_] And for all of that, they still went on Sinning, and did not Believe God's Words of Provable Truths, in spite of his Great Wonders. Therefore, their Days were Consumed with Vanities, and their Years with Troubles — God alone knows how many Troubles, and how many Needless Sufferings. Nevertheless, when he Slew them, then they Sought him, and Prayed to him; and they Returned to the Old Ways of Living, and Enquired Early after God, Praying to him each Morning, Noon, and Night. Yes, they Remembered that God was their Bedrock, and the Most-High God was their Redeemer and Savior. †‡

02-11 [_] Nevertheless, they Flattered God with their Mouths, and Honored him with their Lips, while they Lied to him with their Tongues: because their Hearts were not Right with him, neither were they Steadfast to Keep their Covenant with him: because they were Hypocrites, Liars, Deceivers, and Greedy Hogs, you might say. Yes, they were like Barking Dogs, Stinking Skunks, and Poisonous Snakes, who could not be Trusted. †§‡

02-12 [_] Howbeit, God, being Merciful and Full of Compassion, Forgave their Iniquities, and did not Destroy them; yes, many Times he Turned his Anger Away from them, and did not stir up all of his Wrath, as he could have: beCause he Remembered that they were just Flesh and Bones, being like a Wisp of Wind that passes away, and never returns again, you might say; but, it is not True: beCause all Souls are Recycled, again and again: beCause every Spirit must be brought to Perfection for either Good or Evil, either during this Life or during the next Life: because nothing was Created in Vain. Oh, how often they did Provoke him to Anger in the Wilderness, and Grieve him in the Desert with their Unbelief! Yes, they turned back to their old Sinful Ways, and Tempted God to Destroy them, and Limited the Holy One of Israel, who Wanted to Bless them with Special Gifts, and even make them the Rulers of this World; but, they were never found Worthy of it. Indeed, they did not Remember his Handiwork, nor the Day when he Delivered them from their Enemies. Oh, how he had Worked his Signs in Egypt, and his Wonders in the Field of Zoan; and had turned their Rivers into Blood, and had Flooded them with Lice, Mosquitoes, and Countless Frogs, so that they could not even Drink Water. Yes, he sent Various Kinds of Biting Flies among them, which Devoured them, you might say; and Frogs, which Destroyed the Flies. He gave the Increase of their Crops to the Caterpillars, and their Labors were Consumed by the Locusts, which came in Great Swarms that Darkened the Sky. He Destroyed their Vines with Hailstones, and their Fig Trees with Killing Frosts, and their Date Palms with Worms, with the Hope that they might Honor him for his Goodness. †§‡

02-13 [_] He gave their Cattle to Hailstones, and Killed their Flocks with Hot Thunderbolts. He cast upon them the Fierceness of his Anger, Wrath, Indignation, Hate, Revenge, and Troubles, by Sending Evil Angels among them, even Satan and his Demon Spirits, who Invented Ways to Destroy them. Yes, he made a Way for his Anger and Revenge on them; he did not spare their Souls from Sicknesses, Diseases, nor Deaths; but, he gave their Lives over to the Pestilences, the Plagues, and Heartaches. Moreover, he Smote all of the Firstborn in Egypt, even the Chief of their Strength in the Tabernacles of Ham; but, he made his own Chosen People to go forth like Sheeps, and Guided them through the Wilderness like a Flock of Goats; and he Led them onward in Safety, so that they did not Fear, even while passing through the Bottom of the Red Sea for 3 Months; but, after they passed through it, the Sea Overwhelmed their Enemies, and Drowned them, even Pharaoh and all of his Army with his 600 Iron Chariots, which are still Buried in the Bottom of the Red Sea for a Testimony against them. †§‡

02-14 [_] And he brought them to the Borders of his Sanctuary, even to this Mountain in the Land of Canaan, which his Right Hand had Purchased by the Shedding of Blood, whereby he Cast Out the Heathen Nations from in front of the Children of Israel, and Divided to them an Inheritance by Line and Measure, and made the Tribes of Israel to Live in Tents. However, they were not Contented to Live in Insecure Tents, and Trust God to Protect them. Therefore, they Tempted and Provoked the Most-High God, and did not Keep his Testimonies in their Memories; but, they Turned Back to their Old Sinful Ways, and dealt Unfaithfully with him, even like their Forefathers: beCause they were Turned Aside from the Path of Life, and went Astray like an Arrow that is Shot from a

Deceitful Bow. Indeed, they Provoked him to Anger with their Groves in High Places, where they had Sex Orgies; and they moved him to Jealousy with their Graven Images and with Paintings of Nude People, whom they Worshiped for their Beauty, as if that would Satisfy their Souls. †§‡

02-15 [_] Therefore, when God Heard about it, he was very Angry, and Greatly Abhorred the Israelites, and so much so that he Forsook the Tabernacle of Shiloh, even the Tent that he had Placed among Men; and Delivered his Strength into Captivity, and his Glory into the Enemy's Hands. Yes, he gave his People over to the Sword; and was Angry with his Inheritance on the Earth. Fires consumed their Young Men, and their Maidens were not given in Marriage. Their Priests fell by the Sword; and their Widows made no Lamentations for them: because they could not Respect them for their Whoredoms. †§‡

02-16 [_] So, is that all that you could Tolerate to Translate from that Boring Chapter, O Selected King?

02-17 [_] Well, I Sense that most everyone else is Bored by it; and therefore, I left off at Verse 65. After all, if anyone is Interested in the Remainder of it, they can find it in any *Bible,* which is basically saying that God Rejected Great Britain and America, and Chose the Lying Conniving Edomites to be his Chosen People. †§‡§§ {See www.Amazon.com for: "The New MAGNIFIED Version of the PSALMS of King David!" (The Understandable Version of the Famous Psalms in Plain English!) By The Worldwide People's Revolution!® Book 064.}

02-18 [_] I must Confess that you do have a Strange Sense of Humor, O Selected King. After all, the Zionists are Based in London, New York City and Israel, and they most Certainly Control most of the News Media for most of the World, who are also the Chief Bankers and Money Dealers, Medical Doctors, Lawyers, Chemists, Drug Pushers, Book Publishers, Weapons Manufacturers, Bomb Makers, and so on. Therefore, that Explains WHY C-SPAN Devotes thousands of Hours per Year to Subjects like "National Security," "Homeland Security," "Terrorism," and "Senatorial Hearings" about ISIS, ISIL, and whomever, while neglecting to even Mention World Trade Center (WTC) Tower 7, which Mysteriously Collapsed in less than 7 Seconds, at 5:20 P.M. on September 11th, 2001, in spite of the Fact that no Airplane struck it. (See www.AE911TRUTH.org for the Details.) Indeed, after Years of Begging for a "Hearing" on the *Washington Journal* program,

C-SPAN finally gave in to allowing Richard Gage to have his 15 Minutes in the Spotlight, which should have been an entire Day or 2 of Hearings and Disputing about it. Nevertheless, the Diligent Students are Welcome to Investigate that Subject on YouTube Videos, beginning with the above Link, or **Experts Speak Out,** whereby they will Discover that their False Cover-up Federal Government consists mostly of Ignorant Idiots, or Conspirators of the Worst Kind, who should all be brought to Trial for TREASON, beginning with the President, himself, who is Assisting our Enemies by Aiding and Abetting them. After all, if they have nothing to Hide, why do they not Explain to us just Exactly HOW WTC Tower 7 Collapsed, seeing that there were 283 Hardened Steel Columns (many of which were 22-inches by 52-inches by 47-stories tall) to bring down? Thousands of Architects, Engineers, Physicists, Scientists and Experts from around the World all Agree that no such a Thing was Possible without the use of EXPLOSIVES! ‡ (See Verse 00-30.)

02-19 [_] So, if that is True, why is it not brought to Court? Why is the Evidence not put on Trial? After all, some 30,000 People Lost their Lives over it, most of whom Died from Cancers: beCause of Breathing the Toxic Dust, which was filled with fine Particles of Asbestos. †‡

02-20 [_] I much prefer to read *Psalm 23* — now I lay me down to sleep, and pray the Lord my soul to keep; and if I die before I awake, I pray the Lord my soul to take; but, if I live for other days, I pray the Lord to leave me dismayed: because I have no real interest in learning anything that might cause me to doubt our righteous government, which is the best government in the world, even if it is not perfect, as Howard Zinn proved in his worthless book, called: **"A People's History of the United States,"** which should be gathered up with this book and all other similar literature, and be BURNED: because it is a threat to our national security, which will be obvious to anyone who has the patience to read all of the way to the far end of this sarcastic book, which most definitely proves that Satan ordained medical doctors. †§‡§§

02-21 [_] I was doing quite well with the New Magnified Version (NMV) of *Psalm 78,* until I came to those Outlandish LIES about the Children of Israel passing through the Bottom of the Red Sea at Easy-on-Geber, which was about in the Middle of the Red Sea, from North to South, even as you can Discover on Old Bible Maps, which give the Location of Easy-on-Geber, which was nowhere near to the Gulf of Suez, where False Teachers like to Place the Crossing of the "Red Sea," as if it were not Possible to Cross the Red Sea, itself. However, even crossing the Gulf of Suez would not have been any Minor Undertaking: because the average depth is 40 Meters. However, the Problem with a Crossing anywhere near the Sinai Peninsula is the Fact that there was not any Land along the Sinai Peninsula, where the Israelites might have Pitched their Tents! After all, 6 Million People, Wagons, Horses, Asses, Mules, Camels, and Great Herds of Cattle and Flocks of Sheeps and Goats would have Required lots of SPACE, and not just a narrow strip of land about one-half-mile wide and 20 miles long. (See the Exodus in Wikipedia for the Details.) The Truth is that no one but God knows just WHERE the Crossing of the Red Sea was, if there was any such Crossing at all. After all, no Israelite Encampments have ever been Located, nor any Hebrew Graves ever found, nor any Evidence that might Prove that millions of People ever Lived in that Arid Desert for 40 Years, as the Not-so-Holy Bible proclaims. Indeed, if they did Live there, they must have Refrained from Carving Words into the Rocks: beCause there are no such Words, which would be Highly Unlikely in a Real Situation with Millions of People involved. Even Lewis and Clark took time to Carve their Names in Rocks when they Explored the West, and so did Davy Crocket, Daniel Boone and thousands of Explorers. †§‡

02-22 [_] I want to Learn the Truth about Medical Doctors, and how it was that Moses and Jesus did not Recommend their Services. In Fact, none of the Biblical Prophets Recommended their Services, and at least one Person was Cursed for Seeking their Services. (See *Second Chronicles 16:12* and *Jobe 13:4*.)

— Chapter 03 —

Ancient Medical Care

03-01 [_] One would Naturally Think that the Bible would have a lot to say about Good Health, Medicines, Treatments, and Physicians; but, strangely enough, most of the *Bible* is Devoted to War Games and Religious Nonsense. However, in spite of any Lack of Information, there are KEY Verses that Require a little Study. For Example, in *Psalm 103,* it reads:

"*A Psalm* of David. Bless the LORD, O my soul; And all that is within me, *bless* His holy name! Bless the LORD, O my soul, And forget not all His benefits: Who forgives all your iniquities, Who heals all your diseases, Who redeems your life from destruction, Who crowns you with lovingkindness and tender mercies, Who satisfies your mouth with good *things, So that* your youth is renewed like the eagle's." — New King James Version (NKJV) of Verses 1—5.

03-02 [_] I much prefer the New Living Translation (NLT):

"*A psalm of David.* Let all that I am praise the LORD; with my whole heart, I will praise his holy name. Let all that I am praise the LORD; may I never forget the good things he does for me. He forgives all my sins and **heals all my diseases**. He redeems me from death and crowns me with love and tender mercies. He fills my life with good things. My youth is renewed like the eagle's!" {Emphasis in **bold lettering** are mine.}

03-03 [_] Nothing explains HOW an Eagle's Youth is Renewed. Do Eagles actually become Young again, each Year, each 20 Years, each 40 Years, or what??

03-04 [_] Well, *Jobe 33:25* sheds some Light on that Subject:

"Then his body will become as healthy as a child's, firm and youthful again." — NLT.
A-[_]

"His flesh shall become fresher than the flesh of a child: he shall return to the days of his youth; he shall pray unto God, and he will be favorable unto him; and he shall see his face with joy: for he will render unto man his righteousness. Indeed, he looks upon men, and if any say: 'I have sinned, and perverted that which was right, and it profited me nothing'; God will forgive him and deliver his soul from going into the pit, and his life shall see the light of truth." — Revised New King James Version of *Jobe 33:25—28*.

B-[_] I prefer that Version.

"When a Sick Person becomes so Violently Sick that he or she Prays to God for Help, lest he or she should Die, God may send a Messenger to Enlighten his or her Mind with Inspired Words of Provable Truths, even an Interpreter, one Man among a thousand Wise Men, to Explain WHY Men were Designed to Walk Uprightly, so as to Pick and Eat Sweet Ripe Fruits from Trees, whereby our Bodies can Live in Good Health: because we were Designed to Live in the Garden of Eden. Then God is Gracious to the Repentant Person, and says to the Messenger: *'Deliver him from going down into the Pit: because I have found a Ransom for him. Yes, Feed him with Fresh Raw Sweet Fruits, and Laxative Fruit Juices, until his Bowels are thoroughly Flushed Out, until his Flesh becomes fresher than the Flesh of a Child: because he will Return to the Days of his Youth, when he could Run like a Deer.'* Yes, he will Pray to God, and he will be Favorable unto him; and he will see his Face with Great Joy: because God will render unto him his own Righteousness in Holiness. Therefore, God looks upon Men in their States of Sicknesses, Diseases, and Distresses; and if any of them say, 'I have Sinned, and Perverted that which is Right, and it did not Profit me anything,' then God will Deliver his Soul from going down into the Pit, in the Grave, and his Eyes shall See the Light of Truths, and his Mind will be Enlightened, and his whole Life will be Transformed." — NMV in Plain English. C-[_] I prefer this Version.

03-05 [_] It is WRong to add LIES to the words of God. §

03-06 [_] And what Lies were added?

03-07 [_] The whole thing is one big LIE from the beginning to the end of it. First of all, God has no Messenger to Send to anyone, much less a Messenger who might Enlighten one's Mind with so-called "Provable

Truths": beCause there are NO Provable Truths on this Earth, and especially when it comes to the Evil Events of September 11th, 2001. Secondly, People were not Designed to Walk Uprightly, much less, Pick Fruits from Trees and Bushes: beCause People would need Tails like Monkeys, in order to be Able to do that. However, if a Monkey could be Trained to Harvest Fruits for us, that would be very Helpful. †§‡§§

03-08 [_] It seems that you have made a Liar of yourself, just by Falsely Accusing others of Lying. After all, any Healthy Person on this Earth could Pick Fruits from Trees and Bushes. Therefore, you are the Sarcastic Liar.

03-09 [_] I was just Kidding. I know for a Fact that Verse 03-04-C is by far the Superior Scripture among all Translations, Worldwide. †‡

03-10 [_] ♦♦♦♦♦♦♦ Verse 03-04-C is NOT a Translation; but, it is an Original Inspired Version of *Jobe 33:23—28,* which everyone can now somewhat Understand. However, if you Study the entire Chapter 33, you will Discover that it is "talking" about a Man who got so Sick that he Stopped Eating, even as Job Stopped Eating, and then Elihu Explained what was Happening, beginning in Verse 14, KJV. Yes, Elihu Spoke for God, and God did not Condemn Elihu for it. Therefore, the "Secret" to Good Health was Hidden from the World for thousands of Years, even within the most Studied Book on the Earth, until our Selected King came along to Explain the Mystery, which is now Understandable to anyone who has the Faith to Study it, Carefully and Prayerfully. Yes, if you simply Eat those Sweet Juicy Fruits, your Youth will be Renewed, even as the Eagle gets New Feathers each Year, which the *Bible* calls REGENERATION! And thus, we can be Forgiven and Healed from all of our Diseases, for FREE! †‡

03-11 [_] I am certainly Glad that I had enough Faith to read this far into this Good Book. Otherwise, I might have Remained in the Darkness of Ignorance, and might never have Learned the Truths that can set me Free. However, after my Mind was Enlightened by those Truths, I Attempted to Enlighten the Mind of my Mother-in-law, who Failed to Understand it, who still Fails to Understand it. Therefore, why is that?

03-12 [_] ♦♦♦♦♦ Well, it could be that her Mind is Blinded by Unbelief, Doubts, Fears, and Vain Traditions. After all, most Adult People are now using Drugs; and therefore, they Sincerely Believe that DRUGS will somehow Heal them, or even Save their Lives, in spite of the Fact that all such Drugs are only Deceiving them: beCause, if you Cut your Finger with a Knife, for Example, your Finger has the Power to Heal itself, with or without the Use of any Drugs. Yes, you might have to Wrap the Cut Finger with a Bandage, just to keep it Clean; but, your Body has the Power to Heal itself, without the Use of any Drugs. Otherwise, God would have been a God of Great Injustices: beCause he did not Create any Animals with Hands for Earning Money, whereby they might Buy some Drugs. For Example, the American Buffaloes Roamed on the Great Plains for thousands of Years without the Aid of any Medical Doctors: beCause, if they got Sick or Wounded, their Bodies Healed themselves. †‡

03-13 [_] Can that be Proven in a Courtroom?

03-14 [_] Absolutely. Why not?

03-15 [_] ◆◆◆◆◆◆ No American Judge would Allow such Evidence to be Presented in any Courtroom, whereby Medical Doctors would have to Confess that all Wild Animals Lived for thousands, and perhaps for Millions of Years, without the Assistance of Medical Doctors, even as most of them still Live: beCause they do not Smoke Cigarettes, nor Eat Cooked Foods, nor even Think Evil Thoughts. (At least we Hope not.) Therefore, they are God's Witnesses to the above Provable Truths, who, along with Balaam's Ass, will be Happy to Testify in Favor of those Great Truths during the Day of God's Judgment, when ALL of the Good Books are Opened Up, including this one, which is not Perfect; but, it is Perfectly Good enough for People like us to Learn the Truth from it, which no one has Proven to be WRong. ‡

03-16 [_] So, if Medical Doctors are not Needed, why did Jesus say: *"They who are Whole do not need a Physician; but, they who are Sick. Therefore, I am like a Great Physician, who has not come to call the Righteous People to Repentance; but, the Sinners, who must Change their Ways of Living, and become Holy like the Righteous Ones."* — NMV of *Mark 2:17*?

03-17 [_] Well, is it not Obvious that Jesus Christ is the Great Physician, himself, whose Words of Provable Truths were Mutilated? For Example, he said, *"Except an Unclean Man should Humble himself by Means of Fasting and Praying, until he becomes like an Innocent Child with a Pure Mind and a Clean Body, he shall in no Way Enter Into the Holy Kingdom of All that is Good."* — *NMV of Matthew 18:4*. Things that STINK are Unclean. Ask your Toilet, if you Doubt it. †§‡

03-18 [_] It is more likely that he stated that in another Verse, which was Carefully Removed by Lying Edomites, whose Medical Empire was Threatened by all such Words. After all, Suppose that the Masses of

People should Learn and Obey that Provable Truth — just how long would Medical Doctors stay in Business? ‡

03-19 |_| Chances are that they would all be Out of Business within a Year or 2, if People just Changed their Diets, and began to Eat a "Garden-of-Eden" Diet. However, there would not be enough Fruits to go around. Therefore, that is another Major Problem to Solve. †§‡

03-20 |_| Many Fruits can be Produced in just one Year or 2. For Example, most of the Berries will be Producing within 2 Years from the Time that they are Planted, and they will just keep on Producing more and more Fruits, which is also True for most Grapes, even though they should not be Allowed to Bear Fruits for at least 4 Years, just to Strengthen the Vines. Likewise, Fig Trees can be Planted by the Billions, and thus have lots of Figs within 3 to 4 Years, even if Fruit Tree Houses must be Built over them. Meanwhile, we can Live on Watermelons, Cantaloupes, Honeydew Melons, Squashes, Tomatoes, Kiwi Fruits, Mangos, Apples, Peaches, Pears, Plums, Cherries, Apricots, Bananas, Papayas, Avocadoes, and many other Tropical Fruits. Meanwhile, all Fat People can simply FAST or Stop Eating: because they are like Fat Bears, who can Hibernate until Spring Crops are Growing. Yes, many Kinds of Greens can be Planted during the Fall, including Onions, Garlic, Turnips, Rutabagas, Beets, Swiss Chard, Rhubarb, Cabbages, Lettuces, Celery, Kale, Mustard, Spinach, Collards, Broccoli, Cauliflower, and even Pumpkin Flowers, which are Better than nothing. After all, we are not Limited to Bread nor Potatoes. Wild Greens, like Dandelions, Lambsquarter, and Pokeweed can also be Eaten. The Pokeweed should be Boiled at least 3 times, while dumping the Water off each time. Try to find any other Greens to Eat: because Pokeweed is Poisonous. At least parts of the Plant are. It is the Lazy Gardener's Greens, who may easily Poison himself. I have Eaten hundreds of pounds of Kale with no Bad Effects. {See www.Amazon.com for: "The LUSCIOUS All-Mineral Organic Method of Gardening!" (HOW to Grow DELICIOUS Satisfying Foods for Potential Kingz and Kweenz in Swanky PALACES!), Book 021B, which is a Companion Book of: "Orgimmick Gardening at its Best!" (HOW to Grow Delicious Satisfying Foods without a 10 Million-Dollar Investment!) By The Worldwide People's Revolution!® Book 079, plus: "Poverty Hunger Riots Strikes Brutalities Election Deceptions and Civil Wars!" (The High Price that we Earthlings have Paid for Leaving the Good Land!) By The Worldwide People's Revolution!® Book 014B.}

03-21 [_] A LOT of People would have to take up Gardening, if everyone suddenly Stopped Eating Meats: beCause of being Inspired to do so by some Holy Man, who has the Power of the Gods. However, there is not much Danger in that: beCause the Masses of People have never been Quick to Change their Diets. Even Moses found it Difficult to Persuade the People to Eat Manna for 40 Years; and after that, they went right back to the Flesh Pots of Egypt, you might say. Therefore, it is nothing to Worry ourselves over. However, it is more likely that we will Run Out of Meats to Eat, if the Masses of People do not take up a *"Garden of Eden"* Diet. †‡

{The Man is Literally Starving to DEATH for Enzymes, Vitamins, Minerals, and Good Thots!}

03-22 |_| ◆◆◆◆◆◆◆ I would Bet that not one Person in 10,000 will Change his or her Diet on Account of this Insane Book, which does not even Explain WHY God or Satan HAD to Ordain Medical Doctors. After all, Medical Doctors were Born of Necessities. For Example, our Father had 50+ Horses on his Ranch in Montana, years ago, and one of his Mares got her Hind Leg hung up in a Barbed Wire Fence, and jerked on it, until she cut her Leg right down to the Bone, which anyone could See, if he or she Looked at her, which soon got Infected with Gangrene, whereby her Leg SWELLED UP to twice the Size that it should have been, and the Pus and Gangrene was running out of her Sore Leg. So, guess what she did, being a Wild Horse, who had never even been Caught with a Rope? Well, after a Week or so of being very Sick, she went up on the side of a long sloping Hill, and held up that Sore Leg, and Stood on one Spot for the next 30 Days, while refusing to Eat anything, nor even Drink any Water, which our Father offered to her, and even set some Oats down within 20 feet of her; but, she did not Touch it: beCause she had Obviously LOST her Appetite, even as any very Sick or

47

Wounded Person does. Therefore, her entire Body SHRUNK DOWN, and the Sore Leg also Shrunk Down, until all of the Pus and Gangrene were SQUEEZED OUT of it and into her Bowels. Yes, it is a True-Life Story, my Boy, which can be Proven in a Courtroom, if any of the Witnesses are still Alive; and I am. ‡

03-24 [_] So, how did she get that Pus and Gangrene OUT of her Bowels?

03-25 [_] Well, I just Happened to get up early, one Sunday Morning, in order to Feed 40 or so Cattle before going to Sunday School, and I just Happened to Look Up toward that long sloping Hill; and behold, that Old Black Mare was coming down the Hill, Shaking and Trembling, being nothing but Skin and Bones, you might say, being so Weak that she could Barely Walk. However, she finally made it to the Watering Tank, and began to Sip on the Water, and kept on Sipping for 15 Minutes or more: beCause she was Obviously very THIRSTY, and would have Certainly put a Capital-T on Thirsty: beCause of not Drinking any Water for 30 Days. ‡

03-26 [_] Did she not Bloat UP and DIE?

03-27 [_] Well, she certainly did Fill Up on Water, and so much so that I figured that she would Kill herself: beCause her Sides were really PUFFED OUT; but, she was more Nolijuboul than any Medical Doctor: beCause her Leg was Healed up Perfectly, and so much so that there was not even a Scar left to See! Indeed, I Remembered Seeing the White Bone in her Leg; but, now the Leg was Healed, Perfectly.

03-28 [_] So, what Happened next — did she fall over and DIE, or what??

03-29 [_] Well, she moved away from the Watering Tank a few feet, and began to Nibble on the Dirt; and I Thought to myself, "Why in the World would she be Eating Dirt, when this is Springtime, and there is so much Green Grass to Eat?" But, while I was Thinking about that, she suddenly Humped Up her Back, and Spread Out her Hind Legs, and out of her Anus came a long Stream of Pus and Gangrene and God knows what else, about as big as a Fire Hose, and Shot Out behind her about 15 feet, and landed in a big Puddle!

03-30 [_] And then what Happened? Did she Collapse?

03-31 [_] Well, just as soon as that Waste Matter landed, she Jumped UP into the Air about 4 feet high, and let out a LOUD BELLOW, as if to say: "HALLELUJAH! PRAISE GOD!" And then, when she came back down, she immediately ran up that long sloping Hill — Bucking and Jumping and Running, until she Disappeared over it, and I said to myself, "If she could go without Eating for 30 Days, it is for Sure that those Cattle can go without Eating this Morning," and thus, I ran after her: beCause I was only 10 Years Old, and was used to Running. Therefore, when I found her, she was with the other Mares in that Pasture; but, she was Acting very Strangely: because she would Eat a few Bites of Grass, and then Run away at a certain Distance, Bucking and Jumping and Bellowing something in a Horse Language, or *"Unknown Tongue,"* and thus she came Running back to the other Mares, and ran around them, Nipping at them, and Wanting them to Play with her; but, they would not Play. In Fact, they just Stood there, Dumbfounded, Watching her, as if to say: "What has gotten into you, Old Fool?" But, she had been Physiologically *"Born Again"*! Yes, *"her Flesh was Fresher than that of a Filly, and she had Returned to the Days of her Youth!"* But, the Doctor Knife did not get to Witness it. In Fact, none of my Family nor Relatives got to Witness it: beCause I was the Sole Witness; and you do not have to Believe me, if you so choose; but, your Unbelief will not Change the Facts by even 2.5 Degrees, no matter what you might Believe about it. Yes, you can take it to Court, and Prove it, O Lady Doubtfulness. ‡

03-32 [_] So, was that Old Black Mare never taken to a Medical Doctor nor Veterinarian?

03-33 [_] No, and neither did anyone Catch her, nor give to her a Shot of Pus of any Kind: beCause she was Wild. Moreover, our Dad said that it would Overheat her, if we Tried to Catch her, and that alone might Kill her. Besides that, she had only Costed him 40$; and therefore, if she Died, it was no Great Loss. So, he just left her alone in the Hands of God, even as she would have done 4,000 Years Ago with Moses, when he Fasted on Mount Sinai for 40 Days and 40 Nights, twice in a Row. (See *Deuteronomy 9:9, and 18, KJV.*)

03-34 [_] Oh surely, you do not Believe all such Religious Nonsense, do you?

03-35 [_] I Surely do Believe it, except that I also Believe that Moses took Enemas, which is WHY Joshua went along to Help him with the Water. However, that Part of the Information was left OUT of the Holy

Bible, even though it was Revealed in the Dead Sea Scrolls! Therefore, God has his Strange Ways of Preserving the Truth for us to Learn it, if we are Searching for it. †§‡

— Chapter 04 —

The Doctor Pus Shots and Doctor Pill Popper

04-01 [_] That was an Amazing True-Life Story, O Elected King of "The New **RIGHTEOUS One-World Government!**" (HOW to Establish a **Righteous One-World Government without Going to WAR!**) By The **Worldwide People's Revolution!**® Book 056. Did you not even Inform the Medical World about it?

04-02 [_] No, I was only 10 Years Old, and knew nothing about the Medical World. In Fact, I was Born 40 Miles from their "Horse-spittle," as our Dad used to call it, in the Bull Mountains of Montana, far away from "Civilization," and therefore, Thank God for that. Otherwise, I might have been a Skeptic and Doubter, like that Lady Doubtfulness, who still does not Believe that Story, even though it is True to the Best of my Memory, which is not Perfect by any Means; but, I can still Visualize it in my Mind: beCause it was a very Dramatic Event in my Life, and especially at that Age. I even Remember the Sound of her Voice, and the entire Episode! It Stuck in my Head!

04-03 [_] So, what did your Family Think about it all?

04-04 [_] Well, to be perfectly Honest with you, I did not bother to Tell what I saw to any of them: beCause they were mostly Unbelievers, who had Mocked me for telling other Stories about Things that I saw — such as Flying Saucers or UFOs. Moreover, if *they* could not Believe me, how would anyone else Believe me? Therefore, "MUM" was the Key Word, as Huck Finn might say to Tom Sawyer about "Injun Joe."

04-05 [_] It is more likely that any Stranger would have Believed you, before your own Family would have Believed you. After all, if you ever said or did anything to Cause your Family to Mistrust you in any Way, they would just Naturally Doubt whatever you said, even as you would just Naturally Doubt your own Parents, if they had Taught to you anything about Insanity Clauses coming down Dirty Black Chimneys during Christmas Eve, or Easter Bunnies laying Colored Chocolate Eggs under Plastic Bushes with Imitation Flowers, whereby you would likely Doubt everything that they might Teach to you after that, after Discovering that it is all just a BIG Capitalist LIE, in order to Sell Trash to Ignorant People. But, Worse yet, it is Satan's Way of Breeding Mistrust and Dishonesty. ‡

04-06 [_] So, did you never get an Opportunity to tell some Medical Doctor about the Old Black Mare, whom you call Lucy, and how she got Perfectly Well without the Use of Drugs nor MediSINZ (or Medical Sins) of any Kind? §

04-07 [_] No, I never did Happen to get such an Opportunity; but, now I am putting the Information in this Inspired Book: so that anyone and everyone might Discover it — that is, IF they are Interested in being set Free from the Fetters and Chains of Deceptive Snakes, who come in Various Colors and Kinds, none of whom can be Trusted: beCause they have a Money Motive for most everything that they Say and Do, being similar to most Lawyers, Bankers, Preachers, and Politicians, who Belong to the Synagogue of Satan. ‡ (See *Revelation 2:9 and 3:9.*)

04-08 [_] O Selected King, Trust me, most of the Readers will never Discover that True-Life Story: beCause they will never get through reading *Psalm 78,* which is far too Long and Boring to them. Besides that, they are Turned Off by your Capitalized Words, which is/are not Traditional. However, if your True-Life Story about the Old Black Mare had been put into Chapter 01, a few People might have Discovered it, and a few of them might have Believed it, and even Tried Fasting for a Day or 2; but, just as soon as the Acids in their Stomachs began to Torment them, they would Naturally Imagine that they might be Starving to Death; and therefore, they would just Naturally have to EAT, in spite of Weighing 200 Pounds too much! †§‡

04-09 [_] O Selected King, a Good Editor would put your True-Life Story at the Beginning of the Book, in Chapter 01, where at least some People might Discover it: beCause few People read more than one chapter of any book: beCause of being "Turned Off" by something. After all, there is an "Information Glut," in this World, which is another Trick of the Devil: beCause only the Inspired Words of Provable Truths should be Published, as Moses stated. †§‡

04-10 [_] Well, I am just going by the Leading Guiding Light of the Holy Spirit, who might have a Good Reason for not Wanting me to put all such Information at the Beginning of this Inspired Book. For Example, my Life might be in Danger, if such a Book should become Popular.

04-11 [_] Most likely the Holy Spirit knows that all such Words will be Rejected by most Ignorant People, who will not Believe that a Horse could Live for 30 Days without Eating nor Drinking. Are you Sure that she did not Visit that Watering Tank, every Night, while you were Sleeping? Indeed, what makes you Imagine that you got to Witness a "Miracle," like that? Are you Sure that you were not just having a Dream about the Horse, and did not See anything that she did? I Suspect that you might have been Worried about her, and thus, just Imagined Things about her. †§

04-12 [_] I Suspect that you are just Imagining Things about me and the Horse. After all, a Horse is not a Spiritual Coward, like some People that I know. In Fact, she Experienced the "Horse Cure," which is to "Fast until you get Well, or DIE!" Indeed, if she had been Eating Pizzas, Pies, Cakes, Iced-creams, Candies, and all such Sticky Foods, she would have no doubt DIED from not Eating; but, you must Remember that she had been Living on a Wholesome Natural Diet for a Horse. Therefore, Fasting was a lot easier for her, and a lot less Dangerous than it would be for YOU, O Pig-eating Walrus.

04-13 [_] I am not a Walrus. I am a Psychologist; and I say that you were having a Good Dream, which you eventually came to Believe was a True-Life Story, which you have told to other People for Decades, until now you have come to Believe that it Actually Happened, even though it never Happened, did it?

04-14 [_] I have other Witnesses, who will be Glad to Testify in a Courtroom that it did Happen. Yes, they saw her on the Hillside, and they know that she did not Eat nor Drink for 30 Days. However, none of them got to See what Happened when she Broke her Fast: beCause they were Obviously not Worthy of it; but, God was Dealing with ME, even as he has been ever since I was Born in the Bull Mountains of Montana, just 9 Months after a UFO Visited with my Parents, according to my own Mother, who was not a Liar, which True-Life Story you may also Mock, if you like; but, it will not Change the Facts by even 2.6 Degrees. ‡ {See: **"The Process of Making a RIGHTEOUS KING!" (A Fascinating Autobiography of our Selected King!) Book 082.**}

04-15 [_] So, is it Fair to say that you are a Chosen Son of God, who has some Special Mission in this World of Wonders? Perhaps you are Jesus Christ, Reincarnated? §

04-16 [_] Whatever I am, I am, and you should stop Mocking me: beCause there is a Special Place Prepared for Mockingbirds like you, who shall also be Mocked. †

04-17 [_] ♦♦♦ I would say that such a Person does not Deserve to Live, if he or she Rejects the Great Truths that you Revealed about that Old Black Mare, which are as *Biblical* as *John 3:16*. Yes, it was the Love of God that made it Possible for you to Witness such a Great Event, whereby your own Life has been Saved many Times: beCause of Fasting and Praying. Therefore, I would not Upset myself over anyone's Unbelief. Just Forget it.

04-18 [_] I would say that it is a Good Case to be put on Trial at: "**The GREAT Worldwide TELEVISED Court HEARING!**" Book 041. Yes, everyone in the Whole World should have to Attend that Great Meeting of the Most-Intelligent and Well-Educated Minds, by Means of TVs: so as to Prove the Story to be True or False. After all, if such a Thing Happened ONCE, in Nature, it has most likely Happened many Times. For Example, I had a Dog who got Sick, and thus, Refused to Eat for a couple of Weeks, until he Recovered from it. Moreover, I have Noticed that all Animals stop Eating whenever they get Sick or Badly Wounded. Therefore, I Believe that it is just a Natural Thing, which can be Proven in a Courtroom. ‡

04-19 [_] I say that Huck Finn or Nigger Jim might Believe such a Fairy Tale; but, neither Tom Sawyer, Judge Thatcher, nor any other educated Person would Accept it as being True: beCause there is no Way that any Horse could Live for 30 Days without Drinking Water. †‡

04-20 [_] ♦♦♦♦♦ Well, unlike World Trade Center (WTC) Tower 7, we cannot Prove it by Building another Similar Situation to Experiment with it; but, I dare say that there are many People in this World who will be Happy to Testify in a Courtroom, while under Oath, that they have Witnessed similar Events. After all, was there not some Baby Girl who Survived for 24 Days while Trapped in a Building after an Earthquake? Maybe it was 36 Days? I cannot Recall Exactly; but, I do Remember Hearing about it. Therefore, it is now Time to bring out the Records, and Prove it. †‡

04-21 [_] Do you Sincerely Believe that Medical Doctors will Allow any such Things to be brought into a Courtroom, much less, into "The GREAT Worldwide TELEVISED Court HEARING!" (That Great Meeting of the Most-Intelligent and Well-Educated Minds!) By The Worldwide People's Revolution!® Book 041B? ‡

04-22 [_] Well, if we, the People, DEMAND IT, they will have to Play Ball with us, or else we, the People, will STOP Patronizing them. ‡

04-23 [_] And what makes you Imagine that we, the People, have any Interest in Proving any such Things, since we are only 147 Trillion Dollars in DEBT to the Devil!? †§‡§§

04-24 [_] You should be most Interested in it. Or, is it True that you are in Love with Edomite Bankers, who have Robbed Americans of Trillions of Dollars? {See: "Good Lessons for Honest Wise Men!" (A Simplistic Plan for Totally Solving the Complicated Problems of Deceived Mankind!) By The Smarter Professor of Common Sense! Book 125.}

04-25 [_] ♦♦♦♦♦♦♦ I am the Doctor Pill Popper, and my Daddy is the Doctor Pus Shooter, and neither one of us like the Idea of going to Court concerning this Issue: beCause we Know for a Fact that we would Lose the Case: beCause anyone could Fast for just one Week, and thus, Discover the Benefits that King David was talking about in *Psalm 103,* saying: *"Bless the Lord, O my Soul, and do not Forget any of his Great Benefits, who Forgives all of your Sins, who Heals all of your Sicknesses and Diseases, and who Renews your Youthfulness by Means of Fasting and Praying. Yes, they who Patiently Wait upon the Supreme Ruler by Means of Fasting and Praying shall Renew their Strength, whereby they will Mount Up like the Eagles on Wings of Great Faith! Yes, they will Run all Day long, and not be Weary; and they shall Walk all Night long, and not Faint."* — See *Isaiah 40:31,* KJV. †‡

04-26 [_] That is NOT what the *Scriptures* Teach. See *Matthew 23:23—45.* †§‡

04-27 [_] I am now Ready to take it to Court. Moreover, all of the Righteous People will say a Hearty: "AMEN."

04-28 [_] I Refuse to Check Verse 04-27 with an X of any Color: beCause …

A-[_] I Suffer with Chronic Constipation of the Mind from Eating Alphabet Soup.

B-[_] I am Afraid that I might have to Live a Healthy Happy Life, if the Truth can be Proven in a Courtroom. After all, the Innocent Children will not have any Trouble Believing any such Provable Truths about any Subjects; and therefore, they will Shame us into it, and perhaps even Stop Eating: beCause of their Faith in it.

C-[_] I am Afraid that I might have to Stop Wasting Money on Medications, and even Confess that some of those Medications are EVIL.

D-[_] I am Afraid that I will Die, if I have to Fast and Pray.

E-[_] Anyone can Fast for 3 to 4 Days without Dying; but, if one does not Eat Correctly when Breaking his or her Fast, that could be the Last Break-fast that he or she Eats! Therefore, I am Afraid to Fast. †‡ {See: "The Proper RULES for FASTING!" (The Complete Instruction Manual for True Repentance!) By The Worldwide People's Revolution!® Book 046.}

F-[_] That could possibly be Proven in a Courtroom; but, I am not Brave enough to Handle it. Indeed, I FEAR all such Trials: beCause I might have to Change my Ways of Living, by FORCE of Self-discipline; and I Hate Self-discipline! †§‡

G-[_] I am a Spiritual COWARD, who will have to be Locked Up in some Siberian Prison Camp by the Gestapo SS, before I will Submit to "The Swanky Sword of Divine Truths! (The Most-Powerful Weapon in the Whole Universe!) Book 067. §

H-[_] I Refuse to Check the Box in Verse 04-27: beCause those Edomite Jews might Discover it, whereby they might have me Locked Up in some NAZI Concentration Camp. After all, NA stands for the German National Socialist Worker's Party, and ZI stands for ZIONISTS, who Helped bring about the Establishment of the Israeli State of Zionists, who were Working with Adolf Hitler, who were actually Controlling the Concentration Camps in Europe during the Holocaust: beCause the Zionist Jews did not like the Orthodox Jews, and still do not like them: beCause they are Enemies. Nevertheless, the Zionists can Thank Adolf Hitler for making it Possible for them to Establish the State of Israel, which is WHY that they also Protected Adolf Hitler, and made it Possible for him to Live in Peace in Argentina, until 1968, when he Died at 79 Years of Age! †§‡

I-[_] I Refuse to Check that H Box: beCause I have no Idea what NAZI Stands for; but, if it Stands for the National Socialist Worker's Party of Germany, which brought them Out of the Great Depression in less than 6 Months after Adolf Hitler got Elected, whereby Germany became the Financial Power House of the Whole World, it could not have been all that EVIL. †§‡ (NOTE: You may ~~cross out~~ any Inappropriate Words that you Disagree with, in Order to make any Statement Reed Correctly. Moreover, you may also Add any Appropriate Words to make the Statements Read Correctly.)

J-[_] Justice Demands that we bring all of these Subjects to COURT, and Prove, once and for all Time, WHO is Correct, and WHO has been Lying to us Education Slaves, Work Slaves, Tax Slaves, Interest Slaves, Insurance Slaves, Rent Slaves, Home-owner Slaves, Mortgage Slaves, Food Bills Slaves, Water Bills Slaves, Gas Bills Slaves, Transportation Bills Slaves, Repair Bills Slaves, Telephone Bills Slaves, Entertainment Bills Slaves, Internet Bills Slaves, Doctor Bills Slaves, Hospital Bills Slaves, Drug Slaves, and Childcare Bills Slaves, etc., etc., ETC.! ‡ {See: "Modern Deceived SLAVES!" (10 Simple Steps for Liberating ALL Modern Slaves, Worldwide, Including Yourself!) **By Liberty and Justice for ALL!** Book 113.}

K-[_] If we Elect the Author to be the Supreme Court Judge, and even the KING of **"The New Righteous One-World Government,"** we will get our Justice. Otherwise, we are likely to never get Justice: beCause no Honest White Jew will be in Charge of it. ‡

L-[_] Lots of Laughs! Is your Selected King the ONLY Honest White Jew in this World of Woes? I find that Difficult to Believe, even though I have been Changing my Mind, Lately. †§‡§§

M-[_] Well, if he is not, why is this Book Repressed by the Edomites? Why would they not ALL be Happy to Check Box 04-27? Well, I will tell you why — it is beCAUSE they are Wicked Lying RED Bloodthirsty EDOMITES, whose Chief Motive is Gaining more MONEY: beCause Money is at the Heart of all Capitalist Issues! †‡ {See: 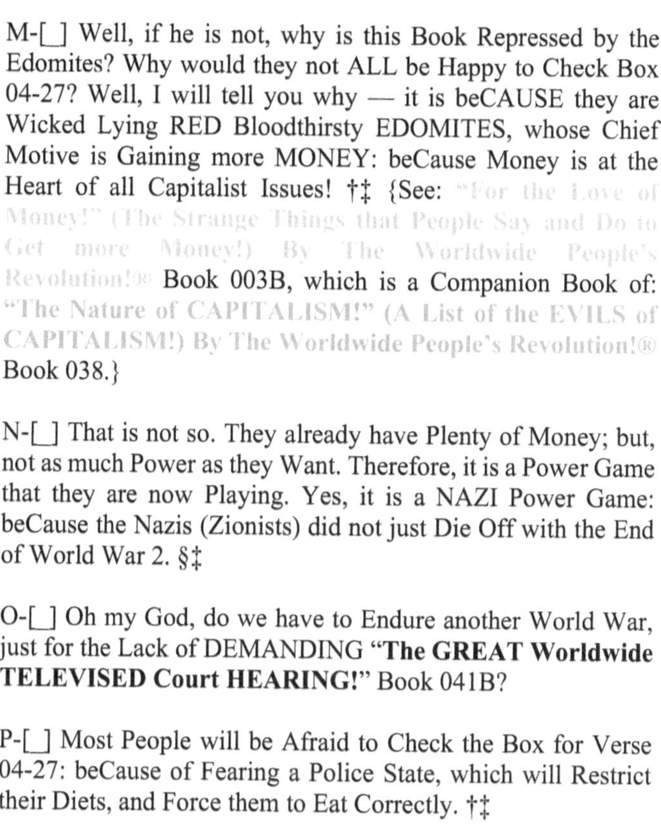"For the Love of Money!" (The Strange Things that People Say and Do to Get more Money!) By The Worldwide People's Revolution!® Book 003B, which is a Companion Book of: "The Nature of CAPITALISM!" (A List of the EVILS of CAPITALISM!) By The Worldwide People's Revolution!® Book 038.}

N-[_] That is not so. They already have Plenty of Money; but, not as much Power as they Want. Therefore, it is a Power Game that they are now Playing. Yes, it is a NAZI Power Game: beCause the Nazis (Zionists) did not just Die Off with the End of World War 2. §‡

O-[_] Oh my God, do we have to Endure another World War, just for the Lack of DEMANDING "The GREAT Worldwide TELEVISED Court HEARING!" Book 041B?

P-[_] Most People will be Afraid to Check the Box for Verse 04-27: beCause of Fearing a Police State, which will Restrict their Diets, and Force them to Eat Correctly. †‡

Q-[_] The Great Question is this: "**Do any of their Fears have any Substance at all?**" Answer: Our Selected King has only Proposed that we all Build Beautiful Self-Governed Planned City States, so that we can Live in Peace with other People of Like-mindedness, so that Good Honest Hardworking Righteous People are not Taxed for Supporting Lying Lazy Sloths nor Criminals of any Kind. Therefore, what is so EVIL about that? ‡

R-[_] The Righteous People are so FEW in Number on this Earth, that a Child might Count them. † (See *Deuteronomy 28:62, KJV,* and Related Verses.) {See: "HOW Righteousness can Overcome Wickedness!" (The Triumph of the Soul who Knows God!) By The Enlightened Professor of Common Sense! Book 093.}

S-[_] The Saints will come Out of the Woodwork when we Hold the GREAT Worldwide TELEVISED Court HEARING. Indeed, they will either come Out and Testify in Favor of the Whole Truth, or else they will be the Last to Enter into the Holy Kingdom of the Gods — be they Jehovah, Yohoovu, Yahweh, YHWH, Allah, Krishna, or whomever.

T-[_] I Testify that your Selected King has it Riit — that there is only ONE Way into that Holy Kingdom, and that is to Pass Through those Pearly White Gates, which Symbolize the PURITY of the True Believers. ‡ {See: "Which Church is the Right Church?" (Can all Churches be Correct?) By The Good Pastor of Uncommon Sense! Book 119.}

U-[_] I Understand what you People are saying; but, I still Refuse to Check the Box for Verse 04-27: beCause my Medical Doctor might Discover it, and have me Silently Murdered. After all, there are no less than an Average of 800,000 to 900,000 Americans, who Die in Hospitals, each Year, and at least 100,000 of them Die from Overdosing on Drugs, or from Consuming the WRong Medications in Bad Combinations, or whatever. †‡

V-[_] Viagra is Safe to Use, unless you Experience an Erection that lasts for more than 4 Hours, in which case you should call your Physician and have him or her Masturbate you. §§

W-[_] WOW, is that all that we have to Do to Handle it? †

X-[_] Well, X-number of People would not know that; but, only Time can get that Poison Out of you. †§‡

Y-[_] I am Yearning for the Time when my Erection never goes Down, even while I am Standing Stark Naked at the Judgment Bar of Almighty God! Yes, what a Glorious Day that will be! †§‡§§

Z-[_] Certain Horny Zebras might Agree with you; but, I would Think that it would be rather Shameful for Bill Adulterous Lying Clinton to be Standing Stark Naked at the Judgment Bar of God, with his Hands Cuffed behind him, so as to not be Able to Point his Finger, and say: "I did not have Sex with that Woman — Miss Lewd-win-skee." §§

04-29 |_| The Righteous People will all be Turned Off with such Talk, and thus, Trash this Book, and all other Literature by your Selected King. Yes, they will Throw Out the Holy Baby with the Dirty Bath Water: beCause, they are just that STUPID! †§‡

04-30 |_| I say that Righteous People will come to Understand that there is only ONE Provable Thing in all of the *Bible,* and that is concerning the Subject of HOLINESS, which is at the Heart of all Biblical Teachings, which is the KEY Doctrine from *Genesis* to *Revelation.* Yes, you too will no doubt Discover it, once your Mind has been Enlightened by Doing some FASTING, Voluntarily, and According to **the Proper RULES for FASTING**. Yes, without Following the Rules, you cannot Expect to Succeed at it. Therefore, do not be an Ignorant Fool. *"Seek, and you shall Find,"* as Jesus stated. And do not be Offended by any Colorful Peacock, even if he is a very Strange Bird. Remember that God Confounds the Worldly-wise People by Means of the Fools in this World, among whom is our Selected King! † (See Books 045 and 046 in Chapter 40.)

— Chapter 05 —

Medical Doctors are Beginning to get Worried!

05-01 |_| Are you Aware of how many Trillions of Dollars are Involved in Medical Care, Hospitals, Drugs, and Insurance — even all of the Medical Industries and Related Services? Well, let me tell you something, O Selected King, those Money-mongers are not likely to Surrender, even if you get them Pinned Down to the Slaughterhouse Floor in a Headlock: beCause they have Great Hopes of Increasing their Businesses, at whatever the Costs and Sacrifices of Lives, which are Expendable to them. †§‡

05-02 [_] Well, it Appears as though they have nothing to Immediately get Worried about: beCause most Americans are Addicted to their Drugs, and are Fully Persuaded that DRUGS are Synonymous with Good Health — as if one could not have Good Health without the Use of Drugs, even though no Wild Animal would Agree with them by any Means, and not one of them Suffers with Human Ailments, unless they get too Close to them. Ask the Wild Mountain Goats, who never Heard of Heart Attacks, Strokes, nor even Arthritis. †‡

05-03 [_] I would like to know why it is that Fasting and Praying is the ONE and ONLY *Biblical* Remedy for whatever might Ail us?

05-04 [_] Well, that is beCause it is Nature's One and Only Cure, and has always been so.

05-05 [_] Are you saying that Animals do not Seek for Special Herbs when they get Sick? I have noticed that my Cat will Nibble on Green Grass, if she gets Sick, which Causes her to Vomit, whereby she is quickly made Well. †‡

05-06 [_] Well, my Friend, Vomiting is just another Way for the Body to Cast Off or Eliminate X-amount of Internal Poisons, which is also the Reason for a Diarrhea, whereby our Bodies Save our Lives: beCause, if that Poison Remained inside of us, it could Kill us. Therefore, we should Thank God for Vomiting and getting Diarrheas. ‡

05-07 [_] So, are you saying that Sicknesses and Diseases are GOOD?

05-08 [_] Well, they are Designed to Save our Lives. For Example, if you Eat some Poisonous Thing, and you Immediately get Sick and Vomit it OUT, that would be Good, would it not? ‡

05-09 [_] Yes, I would say that it would be Good; but, at the Time, it does not Feel very Good — at least not until the Poison is Vomited Out. ‡

05-10 [_] So, the Influenza that everyone is Dreading, is Actually a GOOD Thing, huh?

05-11 [_] Well, if you do not Eat those Slimy Greasy Acid-forming Foods that Provide a Good Foundation for Germs and Bacterias to Build Up in, they cannot make you Sick — at least not for long. Indeed, once your Bowels are Cleaned Out by Fasting and Eating Natural Wholesome Foods, you can Visit People with Influenza, and even "Catch" the Flu for a few Minutes, and Feel a little Sick; but, if your Body is Working Correctly, it will soon "throw it off," as they say: beCause your Immune System is Working Well. ‡

05-12 [_] So, if we were Perfectly Healthy, we would just Naturally be Immune to all Sicknesses and Diseases, huh?

05-13 [_] Well, that was the Case with Jesus Christ. Otherwise, People would have been saying to him, *"O Physician, Heal yourself." — Luke 4:23.*

05-14 [_] So, did Jesus Live on a Natural Wholesome Diet? If so, did he Eat Eggs and Cheese and Candies? §

05-15 [_] Well, the *Bible* is Sorely Lacking any Details about what he Actually Ate, as well as what anyone else was Eating at the Time. The King James Version often Translates "Food" as "Bread" or "Meat." In Fact, one might Think that MEAT was the Staple Diet, which is Suggested in *Genesis 1:29—30.* It should have been Translated as "Food." However, at the Time of King James, MEAT was the Staple Food, and People did not Feel Satisfied without it, even as most Addicted Meat Eaters still Feel, even though Medical Doctors tell them that a Body only needs 3 to 4 Ounces of Flesh per Day for Proteins, or just a little Bowl of Beans with Greens and Fresh Raw Green Onions with a few Raw Nuts, which are quite Satisfying. †‡

05-16 [_] So, our Modern Diet is Basically *Biblical,* huh?

05-16B [_] Not at all. Meat was Eaten on certain Special Occasions, such as Passover and Feast Days; but, normally speaking, Flesh was not Eaten during Biblical Times, and a Limited Amount of Milk, Butter, and Cheese were Eaten: beCause it was also a Luxury for most People at that Time, which is WHY Father Abraham Fed it to Jesus. (See *Genesis 18.*) Whole Wheat Bread was the Staple Diet of the Time, or Barley Cakes and Oats, even though Oats and Rye are not mentioned in the *Bible,* and neither are Rice nor Maize. However, that is not to say that they did not Import Oats and Rye: beCause Shipping Goods was quite Common at the Time of Christ. The Romans had many Ships, and Trading Goods was just as Popular then as now, even though most Foods were Grown at Home, or near their Homes. †‡

05-17 [_] So, is it Fair to say that there were very few Fat People during the Time of Christ?

05-18 [_] Well, there were probably plenty of Heavy People; but, not Blubbery Fat People, like you can see nowadays, whose Legs are

Covered with Cellulite or Adiposis. Most of the People were Poor, and most of them had to Work fairly hard, just to Earn a Living. †

05-19 [_] So, how come there were so many Sick and Diseased People at the Time of Christ, who came to him by the hundreds of thousands? (A bit of an Exaggeration.) †§‡

05-20 [_] Well, they did not have Fresh Fruits to Eat, the Year Around, like we now have. Therefore, they Ate mostly Bread, which is not a very Good Diet. In Fact, the Romans in Italy had a much Better Diet: beCause they Ate more Fruits and Vegetables, including Red Garden Beets and Hot Peppers, which are quite Laxative. The Jews were pretty much "Hung Up" on the Meat, Cheese, and Bread Diet: beCause such Things could be Stored or Eaten before they Spoiled. Salted and Pickled Meats could be Stored for Years, and some Jewish Breads have been kept for as much as 500 Years! †‡

05-21 [_] So, most of the People were Living on Poor Diets, huh?

05-22 [_] Well, most People are still Living on Poor Diets. {See www.Amazon.com for: **"DIETS!" (A Reasonable Solution for the "Eternal Controversy"!), Book 037, plus: "Poverty Hunger Riots Strikes Brutalities Election Deceptions and Civil Wars!" (The High Price that we Earthlings have Paid for Leaving the Good Land!) By The Worldwide People's Revolution!® Book 014B.**}

05-23 [_] So, Medical Doctors really have nothing to Worry about, when it comes to an Eternal Income, huh? After all, 99% of the People are Living on Poor Diets, right?

05-24 [_] Well, it is probably more like 99.999,999% of the People: beCause of all of the Junk Foods, Highly-processed Foods, Poisoned Foods, GMO Foods, and whatever. Not even Rich People have Truly Good Foods to Eat, including the Queen of England! †‡

05-25 [_] So, does God Care?

05-26 [_] Well, he probably Cares; but, it is not his Problem, is it? We made our own Bed, as the old saying goes, and now we have to Sleep in it.

05-27 [_] I say that it is High Time to REMAKE the Bed, and Elect "The New RIGHTEOUS One-World Government!" (HOW to Establish a

Righteous One-World Government without Going to WAR!) Book 056. {See www.Amazon.com for: "The CONSTITUTION for the New RIGHTEOUS One-World Government!" (HOW all Peoples can get True Justice, and Celebrate the Great Year of JUBILEE!) By The Worldwide People's Revolution!® Book 016B.}

05-28 [_] Good Luck!

05-29 [_] You say that as if you had Lost all Hope!

05-30 [_] Actually, I have.

— Chapter 06 —

How the Body Works

06-01 |_| Most People do not know it; but, the Human Body is Basically a PIPE System, having thousands of Miles of Pipes, and Microscopic ones. However, the Main Pipes are from the Mouth to the Anus; and the Lesser Pipes are the Blood Vessels, which run throughout the Body, which Deliver Nutriments to all Parts of the Body. However, like a Sewage Drain in your House, all of those Pipes can get Clogged up with Plaque, Grease, or whatever; or, even Blocked by Blood Clots, which Cause Heart Attacks and Strokes. †‡

06-02 [_] So, is that something that should be Proven in a Courtroom?

06-03 |_| ♦♦♦♦♦♦♦ Well, if you Knew for a Fact that certain Foods were Causing "Roadblocks" in your Bowels, which Cause Chain-reactions, you might Think about Changing your Diet, huh? After all, no one really Likes to Suffer — at least not if they are Sane. Most People pay little or no Attention to what they are Eating, until they get Sick or Diseased; and then they just Naturally go to a Doctor for some Quick Remedy for their Age-old Dietary Sins, while Hoping that they will only have to Consume some "Magic Pill," which will Instantly Cure them from whatever Ails them. However, the Doctor Pill Popper will almost always Prescribe some Medicine or Pills to Consume, and will tell you to be sure to follow the Instructions on the Bottle of Pills, and to come back in a Week for another Visit, or "Checkup": beCause he Knows for a Fact that most Minor Sicknesses will Disappear within a Week to 10 Days, with or without his Pills: beCause he Knows that every Body was Designed to Heal itself, without any MediSINZ. Indeed, even a Dog would know that Fact of Life; but, not all Doctors know it, if no one Informs them of it. It is generally Classified as "Top Secret" Information — somewhat like the President Kennedy Assassination Cover-up, and the 9/11/2001 Covered-up False Flag Operation. †‡ (Kindly Ask George Warmonger Bush and Little Dick Chicanery, Incorporated, just Exactly HOW that Hardened Steel Column Cut Off itself, without the Assistance of Military-grade Nano-Thermite? Notice how quickly they Clam up: beCause, they have no Reasonable Explanation for it, since no Airplanes Struck WTC Tower 7. But, even if a hundred Airplanes Struck such Towers, they could not Cut Off that Steel: beCause, it would be like throwing a Pop Can at a Solid Concrete Wall. But, if anyone Wants to get Serious about it, we can Reconstruct a similar Tower, and Experiment with as many Airplanes as you Like, and Discover that none will Produce Great CLOUDS of DUST!}

06-04 [_] So, what Causes those "Roadblocks" in our Bowels and Blood Vessels?

06-05 [_] Well, that is a very Good Question, which the Doctor Knife has apparently never Discovered, in spite of Cutting into the Bowels to Remove Collections of Lumps, Tumors, Abscesses, Cancers, and whatever. One 40-year-old Woman had swallowed Bubblegum since she was a Child, and the Doctor Knife Discovered some 20 Pounds of Bubblegum in her Bowels, which had Accumulated since she was a Child! But, normally-speaking, those "Roadblocks" are Constructed of Complex Combinations of Foods — such as Pizzas, Hamburgers, Sticky Candies, Pastries, Iced-creams, Eggs, Macaroni, Cheese, Grease, and just about everything and anything that such a Person has been Eating: beCause, if something is STICKY, it is likely to STICK to some other Sticky Stuff, even as Grease in a Frying Pan can Build Up, or even as Grease in a Sink Drain can Accumulate, until the Pipe is Actually Filled Up with it, which calls for Drastic Action to get it OUT with "Drain-O," Lye, Hot Water, and Mechanical Devices in some Cases. However, no one in his nor her Right Mind would put Lye into his nor her Stomach, nor any other Harsh Substance, whereby he or she might get a Diarrhea, and thus, FLUSH OUT his or her Bowels: beCause that would be far too "Radical," even if the "Drain-O" was called "Prune Juice." †§‡§§

06-06 [_] So, it is Obvious that certain Foods are Laxative, while others are Constipating, right?

06-07 [_] Well, if it is not Obvious to someone, such a Person should do a little Experimenting with his or her own Body, and especially if he or she is a Medical Doctor: because some Personal Experience is a Better Teacher than "Second-hand" Lessons from someone like me. Indeed, you only need to go on a Steady Diet of any one Particular Food, in order to Discover just how GOOD it is for you to Eat it. For Example, you can Eat nothing but Watermelons for a Month or 2, and not Suffer with any Constipation. Or, you can Eat nothing but Cheese for a Month or 2, if you are Brave or Foolish enough to do that, and you will most likely Discover what Chronic Constipation is like within less than one Week. Likewise, you could go on a Scrambled Egg Diet for a Week or 2, and Discover the same Evidence of some "Villain in the House." However, to make it more Interesting, you could go on a Cheese Omelet Diet with

Eggs, Bacon, Cheese, and Bread Crumbs fried in Butter and Topped with Peanut Butter, without any Orange Juice, Grape Juice, Apple Juice, nor any other Fruit Juices, lest you should be made Sick by them. ‡

06-08 [_] So, what about a Pure Iced-cream Diet — what would be the End Results of that?

06-09 [_] Well, most likely you would not Die from it; but, you would most likely Contract Lung Diseases, a Sore Throat, Colds, and Mucus Discharges at both Ends. Indeed, it would be a Real Self-inflicted Torment, in my Honest Opinion. Therefore, if you Test any certain Diet, please make a Detailed Record of it, so that you can Present the Evidence at **"The GREAT Worldwide TELEVISED Court HEARING!"** Be Sure to Record all Previous Dietary Habits.

06-10 [_] So, is it not Dangerous to go on Mono Diets? After all, we are not Panda Bears nor Koalas. †‡

06-11 [_] Well, I would not Recommend taking it to Extremes. For Example, if you went on a Red Beet Dict for just one Week, you would likely be Pissing Purple Urine, which could prove to be Bad for your Liver and Kidneys and who knows what else. But, if you went on a Butternut Squash Diet, you would likely not notice any Detrimental Effects from it, even if you Ate nothing but Butternut Squashes and Fresh Green Onions for an entire Year or 2 — that is, IF they were Good Baked Squashes and Raw Onions, which always Tasted Good to you. Indeed, you might want some Olive Oil and Salt on the Steamed Squashes, or Soy Sauce; but, not any Spices: beCause those Spices will work up a Greater Appetite than you Want, and probably Inspire you to Eat at the Death and Hell Restaurant. †§‡

06-12 [_] So, is it Good for us to make Guinea Pigs of ourselves, just to Experiment with Various Unnatural Diets, when Dieticians have been Studying the Subject for Centuries? Why not just Eat a Natural Normal Balanced Diet, according to our Traditions?

06-13 [_] Well, if you are Suffering with Constipation on such a Diet, then it is Equally as BAD as making a Guinea Pig of yourself on some other Bad Diet. One Thing can be Established as a Fact of Life, and that is the Fact that some Foods are less Constipating than other Foods; and the Most Constipating Foods are Things to be Avoided, unless you Want to Suffer with Constipation. I Choose to be Free from it. You may

Choose whatever you Like; but, Try to be Happy with it, and do not Blame anyone else for your Bad Judgments.

06-14 [_] So, suppose that we Choose to go on a Meatless Diet, and contract some Protein Deficiency Disease, who shall we Blame for it?

06-15 [_] Well, you certainly cannot Blame ME for it: beCause I Recommend that everyone should Eat some RAW NUTS, which contain plenty of Fats and Proteins. However, if you think not, then Eat some Beans, Meat, or whatever you Like. Use your Appetite for a Guide. For Example, if you are Craving something, maybe you need to Eat some of it, even if it is Cheese. After all, you will not Eat very much of it before your Appetite is Satisfied for it, if your Bowels are Working Correctly. †‡

06-16 [_] I am Craving someone to Love and have Sex with. Therefore, is there any Food that can Satisfy that Craving? §

06-17 [_] Well, not that I know of. However, if you are not an Attractive Person, you can hardly Expect anyone to Love you. Therefore, Fasting and Praying will Fix that Problem in most Cases; but, not in all Cases. ‡

06-18 [_] Are you Suggesting that those Starving Children in Africa are more Attractive than Fat Children in America?

06-19 [_] Well, that is another Subject. However, even a Child who is Skin and Bones, who is Quiet and Submissive and Peaceful, is more Attractive than a Fat Diseased Child, who is Rebellious, Loud-mouthed and Stubborn. Therefore, you should Experiment with Fasting and Fruit Eating, and Discover if it does not make you more Attractive. Most generally a Youthful Slender Person has no Trouble Discovering someone to Love him or her. However, if you Live an Isolated Life in the Bull Mountains of Montana, you are not likely to Meet anyone to Love. Moreover, even if you do Meet someone whom you might Love, it does not Mean that such a Person is Guaranteed to Love you. Therefore, you can easily set yourself up for Heartaches. ‡

06-20 [_] So, how could we be Guaranteed to Avoid such Heartaches?

06-21 [_] Well, the Surest Way that I know of is for everyone to Fill Out and File "**The Complete SURVEYS of our VALUES!**" (**SURVEYS of Religious Spiritual Political Governmental Sexual Social Moral**

Economical Business Labor Habitual and Miscellaneous VALUES!)
By The Worldwide People's Revolution!® Book 059.

06-22 [_] So, if we have Similar Values as other People, are we more apt to Love them?

06-23 [_] Well, the more you have in Common, the more apt you are to get along well together, I would Think. ‡

06-24 [_] So, would God actually Cause our Life Mate to be Born in some other Country? Does that make any Sense? How many Inconveniences would Result from that?

06-25 [_] Well, I would Think that you are most likely to have more things in Common with your near Naaberz, Friends, and Relatives — and not with someone who is on the other Side of the Earth, which would not be at all Convenient for such Families. ‡

06-26 [_] So, is it Fair to say that it was Satan who Inspired such "Distant Marriages," whereby Families are Separated by thousands of Miles, and are not at all Closely Bonded with each other, being like Strangers on the Streets, whom you might see just once or twice during a Lifetime, which is Extremely Sad. After all, it would be much Better for everyone to have just a few Good Friends and Companions, than to Live in a very Crowded City of Confusion, where no one knows anyone very Well, much less be Able to Trust anyone. ‡

06-27 [_] I have been Hoping to Learn more about the Human Body, and WHY People get Sick and Diseased, so that we might Avoid all such Sicknesses and Diseases.

06-28 [_] Well, if you Sincerely Want to Learn more about your Body, the Best Way to go about Doing that is to FAST or STOP EATING, until all of the FILTH and STINK is Thoroughly Removed from your Entire Body and Mind, which is very Enlightening. Yes, just Do what Jesus Christ said to Do, and Cleanse the Inside of the *"Cup and Platter,"* so that the Outside will also be Clean. In other Words, Clean Out your Mind and Body by Means of Self-denial, by not Thinking any Evil, and by not Eating, until your Body has Cleaned itself. Yes, it is all summed up in these Profound Words of Provable Truths: *"Except an Unclean Man should Humble himself by Means of Fasting and Praying, until he becomes like an Innocent Child with a Pure Mind and a Clean Body, he shall in no Way Enter Into the Holy Kingdom of All that is Good."* —

Jesus. Yes, that is the KEY Verse into the Kingdom! Therefore, Memorize it.

06-29 [_] So, when Moses went up on Mount Sinai, and Fasted for 40 Nights and 40 Days, he was simply Cleansing himself from all Filthiness of the Flesh and Spirit, just as the Apostle Paul wrote about in *Second Corinthians 7:1,* right?

06-30 [_] Yes, that Sums it all up, Perfectly.

— Chapter 07 —

The Chief Sins of Medical Doctors

07-01 [_] ♦♦♦♦♦♦ Many People Worship Medical Doctors, as if they were among the Gods: beCause of "Saving their Lives," they would say. However, Huck Finn and Nigger Jim would now Understand that all such People are Greatly Deceived: beCause Huck and Jim have missed many Meals, and done much Hard Work, just to Survive; and therefore, their Nostrils and Taste Buds Work much more Proficiently than those of Tom Sawyer and FAT Judge Thatcher, who have always been Well Fed, who have never Missed a single Meal since the Time of their Births, except when they got Extremely Sick. However, even during their Sicknesses, their Medical Doctors Recommended that they should be Fed with Sticky Chicken Broth or Beef Broth, Poached Eggs, and Soft Foods like Iced-creams, Jell-O, and Plenty of Liquids — such as Flavored Fruit Juice Drinks, which are made from Recycled Sewage Water, Sugar, Corn Syrup, Preservatives, Imitation Fruit Flavorings, and an entire List of Abominations in fine print, on the backside of the Jug, while on the frontside of the Capitalist Jug it reads: 100% Pure Juice! †§‡

07-02 |_| Is it the Fault of Medical Doctors that Gross Grocery Stores are allowed to Sell all such Abominations to Poor Ignorant People, who cannot Afford to Buy 100% Pure FRESH Fruit Juices, which were Grown on Fruit Trees that were Fertilized with Chemicals, and Sprayed with Deadly Poisons no less than 16 Times, each Year, which Fruits were Washed off in Recycled Sewage Water, and immediately run into Juicing Machines with some of that Filthy Water still on them (or even someone's Spit), and were thus Juiced without Separating the Poisonous Seeds and Rinds from the Fruits, and were then Concentrated by Heating the Juices until they Dehydrated them, and then Froze them and Sent them in Unsanitary Containers to the far Ends of the Earth, where Recycled Sewage Water was Added to the Concentrated Juices, and put into Stinking Cancer-causing Plastic Bottles, and finally set on Grocery Shelves to Sell to Ignorant Fools, who have Lived their entire Lives without ever Tasting of a Good Sweet Fruit that has been Grown by **the LUSCIOUS All-Mineral Organic Method of Gardening!**? Is it not the Responsibility of the Bad Foods and Good Drugs Administration (FDA) to Monitor all such Foods and Drinks? †§‡ {See www.Amazon.com for: "The LUSCIOUS All-Mineral Organic Method of Gardening!" (How to Grow DELICIOUS Satisfying Foods for Potential Kingz and Kweenz in Beautiful Swanky PALACES!) By The Worldwide People's Revolution!® Book 021B.}

07-03 |_| Well, my Sarcastic Friend, the Responsibilities of the Federal Government are Obvious — do whatever is Necessary to get as much Money as Possible into the Hands of Rich Edomites and their Associates, including Medical Doctors, who are some of the Chief Edomites, who Know for a Fact that all such Chemically-grown Foods Cause Cancers, whereby they can Collect Billions of Dollars for "Cancer Research," whereby they can Pretend to be Searching for the CURES for Cancers; but, NOT the CAUSES for them. Indeed, there is an Average of 40,000 Americans who Die in Car Accidents, each Year; and the "Cure" is to make the Cars Safer, they say, rather than get RID of almost all Cars: beCause it is far more Practical to Live without those Stinking Abominations, and thus Live without any Automobile Accidents, and the Diseases that are Produced by Running Cars: beCause of Living within Beautiful Planned City States, which use Electric Elevators, Escalators, and SAFE Subway Trains, whose Tracks are Protected by Thick Stone Walls and Strong Sliding Doors, which Open after the Train has Stopped, which are Designed for Safety and Security. †§‡ {See www.Amazon.com for: "The Right Design for Living!" (A List of Great Advantages for Building Beautiful Planned City States!) By The Worldwide People's Revolution!® Book 012B.}

07-04 |_| So, are you saying that our Good Fatherly Loving Federal Government does not Actually Care for our Good Health, and is only Seeking the Wealth of Rich Hogs, Drug Companies, False Medical Doctors, Edomite Bankers, Evil Chemical Corporations, Weapons Manufacturers, and a whole List of EVILDOERS? Are you asking us to Lose Faith in such a RIGHTEOUS Government, which Wastes HUNDREDS of BILLIONS of Dollars per Year on Medical RESEARCH, which is like the Fox Investigating the Murders in the Chicken House, as they say? Surely they Love our Souls! Remember 9/11/2001, when the so-called "Greatest Air Force in the World" was Helpless to Save us from Hijackers with Box Cutters, who let the "most Secured Building in the World" be Attacked, at the Pentagon, in the very Spot that was made most Secure at a Great Expense of Millions of Tax Dollars, which "Airplane" did not even Break Out the Windows where the Wings supposedly Crashed into it with their 6-ton Titanium Jet Engines, which were never Found! †§‡§§ {See: *Pilots Speak Out* and *Experts Speak Out,* on YouTube Videos; or just Study www.AE911TRUTH.org for the Proof of a False Flag Operation. Guaranteed. See Dr. Judy Wood's Videos. Bankers, Doctors, and Weapons Manufacturers gained more than 6 Trillion Dollars from it all. Not a Bad Profit, huh? And WHO will Pay for it all? American Tax Slaves, Interest Slaves, Insurance Slaves, Drug Slaves, and Work Slaves, who still Pledge their Allegiance to their American Rag: beCause, they are so PROUD to be Americans, who should Study: "C-SPAN-DEX!" (Your Filtered View of Bad Government!) By The Worldwide

People's Revolution!® Book 097 and, "The Great ATOMIC NIGHTMARE!" (The Saddest Story in World History!) By The Great White Bald Eagle! Book 099!}

07-05 |_| Surely they do NOT Love our Souls. What they Love is MONEY, no matter HOW they have to get it; and they are Certainly NOT Interested in Proving anything in a Courtroom, if it Threatens the Revenues of those Wicked Lying Zionist EDOMITES, who are the Chief Sinners! Yes, it might come as a Shock to most Americans; but, not to the Remainder of the People of the World, who are getting Educated by Means of the Internet, who are Catching On to the Deceptive Tricks of those Lying Warmongering Edomites, who are Good at Discovering the Slivers in the Eyes of other People — such as the Iranians — while Ignoring the LOGS in their own Eyes, which are Blinding them from Seeing the Truths about themselves. †‡ (Go to YouTube and Search for "Benjamin Freedman," who was an Honest White Jew, like me.)

07-06 |_| So, are you saying that if a Medical Doctor does 15 Minutes of Surgery on someone, that he or she is not Worthy of 60,000$ for that Operation? Are you Suggesting that an Unsanitary Hospital Room is not Worth 3,000$ per Day, when the Best Hotel Room in Town would not be half that Price, and come with Hot and Cold Running Maids? †§‡§§

07-07 |_| ♦♦♦ Well, it is True that Hospital Rooms are Designed for the Benefits of Patients, and are Good Places to Contract Diseases from Germs that are Floating all about in Air Ducts, which are never Cleaned, which are more Dangerous than the Air Ducts in Normal Hotels: beCause Hospitals are Filled with Sick and Diseased People; but, when People are Eating Unnatural Unwholesome Foods and Drinks, what else can they Do, except to Play Russian Roulette, and Commit themselves to all such Hospitals, where Loving Smiling Medical Doctors can Obtain all of the Patient's Money in their Bank Accounts just before they Die? Indeed, why Mess Up such a Profitable Business by Publishing the Whole Truth in Public Schools? Why not Feed Sticky Candies to Ignorant Children, so as to Rot Out their Precious Teeths, whereby they will need the "Services" of Dentists, for Example? Take Note that Remote Jungle Tribes in Africa have Perfect Teeth without any Dentists, even as the American Bisons also had Perfect Teeths. †§‡

07-08 [_] God have Mercy, O Elected King, you are not giving any Slack to those Witchdoctors, at all, are you? Why do you not bring all of them to Court, and Prove them to be Guilty of Covering Up the WHOLE Truth about themselves, whereby you can Lop Off their Heads with "The Swanky Sword of Divine Truths!" Book 067? †§‡§§

07-09 [_] Well, that is Exactly what I Intend to Do, if the Masses of People will Help me to Do it.

07-10 [_] Boy, O Boy, I would sure Hate to be one of those Red-eared Medical Doctors in your Courtroom! Yes, that would Prove to be very Em-bare-assing, I must say. After all, any Number of Honest Medical Doctors could be Locked Up in Comfortable Jail Cells, and Fed nothing but Tasty Velveeta Cheese for one Week, and thus "Catch" the Common Cold, and thus Prove that it does Matter what we EAT! Yes, our DIETS are the Chief Sources for our Sicknesses and Diseases; and any Person with a Rational Mind would Know that Fact of Life, in spite of anything that was supposedly said by Jesus Christ, who supposedly said: *"It is not that which Enters Into a Man's Mouth that Defiles him, so much as that which comes Out of his Mouth, which comes from a Vile Mind and Unclean Bowels. Yes, such a Person must Change his Thinking, and Stop Thinking Evil, whereby he will Develop an Appetite for Eating Good Sweet Fruits, while the Evil-minded Person will Develop an Appetite for Eating all Kinds of Unclean and Forbidden Foods, whereby he is Overcome by them: beCause of becoming Addicted to all such Addictive Foods."* — The Gospel According to Saint Addiction! †§‡§§

07-11 [_] You will do Well to Meditate on those Inspired Words of Provable Truths, before you are put into an Uncomfortable Prison Cell with Lying Edomites, who Deny the Truths of it, who Teach Outlandish LIES — such as that Lie about "all Meats were made Clean," which is Translated as "all Foods were made Clean," when those Ignorant People, 2,000+ Years Ago, did not have any Idea what People would be Eating during the Future, much less the Fact that some Wicked Anti-Christ FALSE Cover-up Federal Government would be in Charge of them, and Promote the Sales of Candies, Cookies, Cakes, Cokes, and other Tooth-rotting Abominations: beCause of being able to Collect Taxes on such Sales, which is also WHY they Allow the Sales of Tobacco Products: beCause of the Love of MONEY, Chemical Preservatives, Slaves and so on! †§‡

07-12 [_] God have Mercy on them, O Selected King, if you get in Command. However, you would have to be more than a Powerless President, in Order to make any Proper Changes. Indeed, you would have to be an Elected KING of Kings, and RULER of Rulers, who has Authority to make Proper Changes, and to Punish those People who do not Submit to the Sword of Truths! Yes, after those Medical Doctors Deny that Velveeta Cheese will give to them Common Colds within a Week or 2, you can have them Locked Up in Comfortable Jail Cells with Exercise Equipment, and get them Converted to the Truth by Means of a Realistic, Scientific Experiment, whereby ALL of them will "Catch" the Common Cold, and have Snot Running Out of their Noses, just as the Children of Israel Experienced in the Wilderness of Temptations and Sins, when they Ate Quails until the Snot Ran Out of their Noses, just as Moses Reported in *Numbers 11,* King James Version (KJV)! †§‡ {See: "Swanky Institutions for Compassionate Corrections!" (How to Correct even the Most-Stubborn Bullies!) **By The Biggest Bully of All Bullies! Book 116.**}

07-13 |_| Well, my Friend, those Chief Medical Cheaters might not like it; but, if they are not Willing to Experiment on their own Willpower, then we will be Forced to Prove it to them by Locking them in Jail Cells, whereby we can Control their Diets, and Monitor them with TV Cameras, 24-hours per Day, so that everyone in the World can Observe and Learn some Good Lessons from them, who will have to Confess that the Volunteer Fruit-eating "Inmates" in the Jail Cells next to them are not Effected by the Slime in their Nostrils! Yes, they will not "Catch" any "Colds," nor show any Symptoms of being Sick: beCause of having Good Diets — Plain and Simple. †‡ {See: "Beautiful Swanky FASTING SANITARIUMS!" (HOW to Learn Good Self-Discipline!) **By The Worldwide People's Revolution!® Book 115.**}

07-14 |_| ♦♦ Awe, I now Understand WHY you formed "The Worldwide People's Revolution!" (A Comprehensive Plan for Obtaining Worldwide Law, Order, Obedience, Peace and True Prosperity!) By The Worldwide People's Revolution!® Book 108, O Selected King. What a Great Idea! I can hardly wait for that Experiment to be Conducted, just to Prove that those Trillions of Dollars have been *Wasted* on Medical RESEARCHES, which were not even Scientific! After all, when it comes to Good Health, one would have to Ask: **"WHY are no Wild Animals Suffering with Human Diseases, unless they come into Contact with Human Abominations?"** Yes, most of the Wild Animals Live their entire Lives without "Catching Colds," for Example. However, if they do get Sick, they simply STOP EATING until they get Well again: beCause that is a Universal LAW that they Follow Faithfully, which can be and should be and will be Proven in your Courtroom! †‡

07-15 [_] Now I Understand WHY Moses said that no one should Add nor Detract anything from his Words: beCause all such Words as these could be Perverted by Dishonest Medical Doctors, and especially if they were in Charge of Translating *Matthew 15:16—20.*

07-16 [_] So, it seems that the World has been Perverted by the Mistranslations of the *Holy Bible,* right? {See: "The Sixth Book of Moses called GOOD GOVERNMENT!" (The Primary Missing Book in the Holy Bible!) **By The Worldwide People's Revolution!®** Book 126.}

07-17 [_] Well, it was a Critical Move by Satan, himself, who had to make Sure that the Masses of People were Misled by Mistranslations, which are Concluded by *Revelation 22:18—19,* whereby no one Dares to Add any Truths to it, nor Reveal any Lies in it. †‡

07-18 [_] So, did God Know that he could Raise Up an Honest Man during the Future, who could Reveal the Whole Truth to all of the People concerning all Important Subjects; and therefore, if only a Portion of the Truths were Preserved, that would be Sufficient Information to Enlighten his Mind, whereby all such Things could be Straightened Out?

07-19 [_] Yes, God Knew it; and therefore, he Preserved just enough Information for me to be Able to Figure it all out, whereby I have Written many Inspired Books for your Enlightenment. †‡

07-20 [_] Suppose Satan is Working through you, misleading us, once again? Indeed, HOW can we Prove your Words to be True or False??

07-21 [_] ♦♦♦ Well, for Beginners, you can Buy a large Package of that Tasty Velveeta Cheese, whereby you can Prove that it is Possible for you to "Catch a Cold" by Eating it; and you can also Recover from it by FASTING and Eating Fresh Sweet Raw FRUITS, until your Bowels are FLUSHED OUT, just like the Sewage System that gets Clogged up with FILTH and STINK, which must be FLUSHED OUT, now and then. †‡ (See *Velveeta* in *Wikipedia* on the Internet.)

07-22 [_] So, if Medical Doctors are not Willing to Experiment with their own Bodies, should they be FORCED to Experiment by Orders of the Court? Would that be Freedom of Speech, or what? Would that not be Transgressing their CIVIL RIGHTS? †§‡

07-23 [_] ◆◆◆◆◆◆◆ Well, they are the Unholy Ones who have set themselves up as Authority Figures concerning Medical Care, who have taken it upon themselves to Administer Shots of Pus, Pills, and Doctor Bills; and therefore, they should be brought to Court, and made to Prove to us that our DIETS are NOT the Determining Factors concerning Good Health and Bad Health. Indeed, it is one of those Things that is EASY to Prove in a Courtroom. Moreover, they have made the Masses of People into their Guinea Pigs for Decades, at our Expense, while making themselves RICH, while Robbing us. Therefore, it is now Time to bring their Evil Empire to an END! †‡

07-24 [_] So, will the Politicians go along with that Plan, and Order them to Court?

07-25 [_] ◆◆◆◆◆◆ Now, pray tell, WHY would they Do that? Indeed, that would be Bad for their Business: beCause they Collect a LOT of Money from the Sales of Drugs. In Fact, it is, and has been, one of the largest American Businesses, since the Time of Father George Washington, who was the First Drug Addict, who Grew and Sold Tobacco, who Grew Grains and Sold Whiskey, whose Livelihood Depended on the ADDICTIONS of Drug Slaves! Therefore, the Nation was Founded on DRUGS, Deceptions, and Satanic LIES — such as all Men being Born Equal with Jesus Christ and Moses! †‡ (See *Numbers 16* for "Equal Rights" and "Civil Deceptions.")

07-26 [_] God have Mercy, O Selected King! If what you say is True, this Nation is "the Great Satan," just as the Iranians have said! Moreover, Israel is "the Little Satan": beCause its Chief Income also comes from the Sales of Drugs and Weapons! Therefore, it is now Understandable WHY they are forever Beating on the War Drums: beCause it is BIG Business, even TRILLIONS of Dollars-worth of Business! †§‡

07-27 [_] Can all of that be Proven in a Courtroom, O Selected King?

07-28 [_] Absolutely! It MUST be Proven in a Courtroom, and that Great Trial must be Published Worldwide on ALL Channels on ALL TV Networks in ALL Major Languages: so that everyone in the Whole World might Learn from it, and come to Understand the NEED for Building those **"GLORIOUS Swanky Hotels Castles and Fortresses!" (Beautiful Planned City States for WISE Intelligent Well-Educated People with Common Sense and Good Understanding!) By The Worldwide People's Revolution!® Book 019B, which is a Companion Book of: "LIGHTNING STRIKES**

Versus Lightning Bugs!" (HOW you can Become Moderately RICH, without Telling any Lies nor Selling any Trash!) By The Worldwide People's Revolution!® Book 074. Yes, it is now Time for almost all People to become Moderately RICH, and by Means of only 6 Years of Common Skilled Labor, by Working only 4 Hours per Workday, 6 Days per Week, or the Equivalent thereof! †‡ {See www.Amazon.com for: **"The Low Court of Supreme Injustices is Brought to Trial!" (Our Elected King Butts Heads with the United States Supreme Court, with or without their Black Robes of Hypocrisies and Lies!) By The Worldwide People's Revolution!®** Book 011B.}

07-29 [_] So, just Exactly HOW are we going to Persuade the Masses of People in this World of Woes to DEMAND **"The GREAT Worldwide TELEVISED Court HEARING,"** seeing that we do not Control the News Media, the Movie Productions, the TV Networks, the Radios, nor even the Newspapers and Magazines?

07-30 [_] ♦♦♦♦♦♦♦ Well, Thank God that Velveeta Cheese is CHEAP, whereby almost everyone in the World can Afford to Buy a large Package of it, or even 3 large Packages, if they have a Family, whereby they can Personally Experiment with "Catching a Cold," which Medical Doctors have not yet Discovered: beCause of being Spiritual COWARDS, who are Afraid to Experiment with their own Bodies. After all, such Cheese does Taste Good, and it is the Perfect Slimy Diet to Prove my Point — that is, if you Eat nothing but that Cheese for a Week or 2, until you "Catch" the Cold, in spite of being Isolated in your own House, so as to not Imagine that you Actually "Caught" the Cold from some Friend or Naaber. Indeed, you may Quarantine yourself, and thus be Scientific about it, and soon Prove my Words to be [_] True or [_] False, just by a Simple Experiment, which any Medical Doctor could also Do, if he were not a Spiritual COWARD! Therefore, after you have "Caught" the Cold, it is Time to "Cure" yourself from it within the next Week, by simply Flushing Out your Bowels with some of that Poisonous 100% Pure Fresh Orange Juice, after Fasting for just ONE Day, which any Brave Soul can Accomplish, even if he or she is just a Spiritual Coward, and then go on Fasting on nothing but Pure Water for the next Week; and then Drink another Gallon or 2 of that Fresh 100% Pure Orange Juice, so as to FLUSH OUT your Bowels, once again, whereby most of the Cheese will be Flushed Out of your Body; but, if it is not all Flushed Out, you only need to Fast for another Week or 2, until it is Flushed Out, along with whatever other Stink and Filth might have Accumulated within your Body, whereby your Mind will be Greatly Enlightened, and so much so that no Medical Doctor will ever be Able to Sell any more Drugs to YOU. Meanwhile, you will be Laughing all of the Way to the Bank, while he will be Scratching Cheese and Grease on his Head: beCause the Body must Try to get Rid of it, somewhere, even if it Sweats it Out through the Pores of the Skin. Indeed, if you cannot go a whole Week without taking a Shower, and without Itching from the Filth that is coming Out of you, and without Stinking, it is beCause you have Completely FAILED to Understand *John 13:10*, NMV. †‡

{When and if they ever get Sick, they Lose their Appetites, which Causes them to Stop Eating, until they get over it. Wise People can do the same Thing to get Rid of the Bug-19. Guaranteed. But, you must Follow: **"The Proper RULES for FASTING!"** (**The Complete Instruction Manual for True Repentance!**) **By The Worldwide People's Revolution!®** Book 046, otherwise, you could KILL your Ignorant Self. Remember the Words of King Solomon: *"Do all Things with True Nolij, and do not Presume that you Know anything; but, Assume that you know nothing yet, as you ought to Know." — The Acts of King Solomon, First and Last.* Obey your own Body, and do not Listen to any Snakes with Poisons in their Heads. If it does not Taste Good, do not Eat it. Remember the Garden of Eden, which is the Garden of Good Eating.}

— Chapter 08 —

"He that is Internally Washed Clean, needs not to ..."

08-01 |_| ♦♦♦♦♦♦♦ Awe, I see that a KEY Word was Deleted from the King James Version (KJV), which is "Internally," which Unlocks the Mystery of the entire Verse: *"Then Jesus arose after Supper, and laid aside all of his Garments; and took a large Towel, and Girded himself with it. After that he poured Water into a Basin, and began to Wash the Disciples' Feets, and to Wipe them Dry with the Towel by which he was Girded. Then he comes to Simon Peter, who said to him: 'O Ruler, why do you Wash my Feet?' Jesus Answered him, "What I do, you know not; but, you will know hereafter, when you Learn the Truth about it.' Peter said to him, 'You shall never Wash my Feet: because I am unworthy of it. Indeed, I should be Washing your Feet. Therefore, why do you want to Wash our Feets?' Jesus Answered him, 'If I do not Wash your Feets, you will have no Inheritance with me in the Holy Kingdom of All that is Good.' Simon Peter said to him, 'O Ruler, in that Case, do not Wash my Feet, only; but, also my Hands and my Head — yes, Wash my entire Body: because I am Unclean, and Smell like a Dead Fish: beCause I have been Eating Fishes.' Then Jesus said to him, 'He who has been Internally Washed Clean does not need to be Washed, except for his Hands and Feet: because he is every bit Clean, even as I am Clean, and even as you would also be Clean, if you did enough Fasting, and Feasting on Sweet Fruits between Fasts. Nevertheless, there is one among you who has an Unclean Heart, which only God can Cleanse, if he Wants to. However, he does not Want to: beCause he has a Special Mission to Fulfill, who was Appointed for that Purpose before he was Born, and he will Betray my Trust in him: beCause he is a Betrayer of Trust, even as the False Physicians are also Betrayers of Truths and Trusts for the Sake of Gaining Money. After all, they could Teach the Truth to the Masses of People about HOW to Obtain and Maintain Good Health; but, that would not be in their Financial Interest, when it is much more Profitable for them to Sell their Drugs, Lotions and Potions, while Pretending to be Good Trustworthy People, even as Witchdoctors have done in Africa for Centuries, whereby they have Robbed the People by Deceptions and Lies.' And thus, Jesus Explained to his Disciples what was Revealed in Numbers 11, Psalm 78, Jobe 33, and Isaiah 40:31."* †§‡

08-02 [_] That was most Enlightening to my Mind, O Elected King. However, it is NOT a Quote from any *Bible*. ‡

08-03 [_] Well, you are WRong about that: beCause it is a Quote from *the New MAGNIFIED Version (NMV)*, which is the *Authorized Version* that God Loves: beCause it is Revealing the TRUTH about it, which no one has Proven to be WRong by any Means. †‡

08-04 [_] So, why do you say "Feets," instead of Feet? Is that not Bad English?

08-05 [_] Well, there are the Feet of Peter and the Feet of John and the Feet of James, and so on, which makes many Feets, even as we have many Peoples, such as the Chinese People, the Indian People, the American People, and so on. Therefore, it is a Proper Use of the Plural Form of the Word with an S, even if it is not Traditional to do so: beCause it is Riit. Take me to Court, and we will Prove it, and Conform to whatever is RIIT. †‡

08-06 [_] I noticed how you used an S on Sheeps and Bisons, which does not Sound Correct; but, Technically, you are Correct — all Plural Words should have S's on them, just to Avoid any Confusions in the Minds of the Childrens, who have been Conversing with the Cherubims on other Earths. Yes, **"All of the Arguments are in Favor of our Selected King, who has Zero Challengers!" (Before you Attend another Election Deception, you should Carefully Study this Inspired Book with an Honest Open Mind!) By The Worldwide People's Revolution!®** Book 085. †§‡

08-07 [_] When Satan Confounded all of the Languages, he did a Royal Job of it, huh?

08-08 [_] According to the *Bible,* it was GOD who Confounded all of the Languages, even though the Bible clearly States that *"God is not the Author of Confusion."* — A part of *First Corinthians 14:33, and 40,* RKJV. (If you Agree, please Check the Box.)

08-09 [_] ♦♦♦♦♦♦♦ So, from now on, when we Discover "Elohim" in the Original Hebrew, we should Translate that Title as "Gods," riit? For Example, in Verse 1 of *Genesis 1,* it uses "Elooheem" for Gods, like this: *"In the Beginning, billions of Years Ago, the Gods Created the Heavens and the Earths, Spiritually, without Number, before they Naturally came into Existence, being as Numerable as the Grains of Sand on the*

Seashores, which now Stretch Out forever and ever, Physically: beCause there is no End to them, even in a Great Multitude of Countless Universes. And thus, the Earths and all of the Worlds were without any Forms, having no Physical Bodies: beCause everything was Void and Empty, and Thick Darkness was in all of Deep Space: beCause there was no Light; but, there was Waters or Gases; and the Spirits of the Gods Moved on the Surface of the Waters. And then the Most-High God said, 'Let there be Light,' and there was Light, even as he Spoke: beCause everything Obeyed his Voice: beCause he is All that is Good, while Satan is All that is Evil, and the Father of all Lies, Deceptions, Crimes, Wars, Plagues, Sicknesses, Diseases, Adulteries, Rapes, Lusts, Greed, Envy, Hate, Murder, and all such Evil Things, who Inspires People to Say and Do Evil Things: beCause the Spirits of all Peoples must be Tested in the Furnace of Afflictions, just for the Gods to Discover which Souls are Worthy to Govern those Endless Worlds, each of which were Created Differently: beCause no 2 Worlds are just Alike, even as no 2 Gods are just Exactly Alike: beCause all of the Gods Love Diversities, as well as Uniformities. For Example, each Kind of Flower is Unique and most Beautiful when Standing with the same Kind, in Uniformity, even as the Flocks of Birds, Schools of Fishes, Holy Angels, and all such Families. And the Gods saw the Light, that it was Good; and the Gods Divided the Light from the Darkness, and put Satan in Charge of the Works of Darkness: beCause he had a Rebellious Spirit, being Puffed Up with Great Pride for his Marvelous Beauty: because he was the most Beautiful Angel that the Gods had Created, who had no Right to be Proud of his Beauty: beCause he did not Create himself, nor any Good Thing; but, he became the Inventor of Evil Things, whereby all Souls might be Tested for their Goodness or Evilness; and thus the Gods called the Light, Daylight; and the Darkness they called Night, and put Satan in Charge of it, who is Symbolized by the Inconsistent Moonlight, whose Light is Forever Changing, who is a False Reflection of the True Light, which is the Sunstar, which Symbolizes the Anointed Savior of this World, who is the Chosen Son of the Hebrew God, called Yohoovu God, who Livz Inside of Jupiter, who is the Father of Mankind. And thus, the Evening and the Morning was the First Great Day of Creation, which was a thousand of our Years: beCause it Required Time for the Gods to get everything Planned and Organized." — NMV.

08-10 [_] So, is that Actually what Happened in the Beginning? Was the entire Universe filled with GASES or "Waters"; and, if so, WHERE did the Gases come from?

08-11 [_] Well, *Genesis* does not Explain all of that; but, you can Believe that it is Correct at the Core of it. †‡

08-12 [_] So, how could that be Proven in a Courtroom?

08-13 [_] Well, all Honest Scientists and Astronomers will Confess that Sunstars are still being Born: beCause everything is still Multiplying, even in its Strange Way. Therefore, it is a very Marvelous World, when you Think about it. Indeed, any Honest Medical Doctor Realizes that Fact: beCause the Human Body and Mind is still a Mystery to them, or else they would at least Understand HOW to "Catch a Cold" by Eating those Things that make it Possible for the "Cold" to Form, even as the "Waters" made it Possible for the Earths to Form, and most of them are Hollow, having more Life on the Inside, than on the Outside: beCause of having less Water on the Inside, and more Land. Yes, it is the most Beautiful Part of this World, also: beCause the Holy Kingdom of our God is on the Inside. See *Luke 17:21, Psalms 48, 50, and 87,* NMV. Yes, Glorious Things are Spoken of you, O Mount Zion, O Holy City of the Most-High God. †‡ (NOTE: Jerusalem is the Wayward DAUGHTER of Zion — not Zion, itself. See *Psalm 9:14; Isaiah 1:8; 10:32; 37:22; 52:2; 62:11; Jeremiah 4:31; 6:2; Lamentations 1:6; 2:1, 4, 8, 10; 4:22; Micah 1:13; 4:8, 10; Zephaniah 3:14; Zechariah 2:10 and 9:9.*) {See www.Amazon.com for: **"The Secret City of the Great King!" (HOW the True Church will Escape from the Great Tribulation!) By The Worldwide People's Revolution!® Book 042.**}

08-14 [_] So, do all of those Holy People Understand the Lies and Deceptions of Medical Doctors? And, if so, why do they not come over here and set things Straight? Why do they allow Mankind to go on Suffering?

08-15 [_] ♦♦♦ Well, Nature must "Run its Course," as they say, just for the Gods to Discover WHO is Worthy to Govern this World of Wonders. After all, would you Want some Lying Snake or Stinking Skunk in your Kingdom, if you were Trying to Establish a RIGHTEOUS Kingdom? Remember that the Symbol for Medical Doctors is 2 Snakes Kissing each other while Wrapped Around a Sword, which is the Perfect Symbol for them: beCause they are like both Poisonous and Harmless Snakes. Indeed, one is Poisonous, and the other one is not; but, they are still Kissing each other: beCause they are in Agreement with each other, since their Goal is to Obtain as much Money as Possible, no matter who might have to Suffer for it. Otherwise, their Medical Assistance would be Free, even as mine is Free, says the Master Farmer and Chief Agitator! †§‡

08-16 [_] So, are you not Afraid that those Snakes will Conspire to Murder you, O Elected King?

08-17 [_] No, I am not at all Afraid of it: beCause it has been Revealed to me that I will be Dead, before they Discover my Inspired Words of Provable Truths, whereby I will Escape, which is very Comforting to me. †§‡

08-18 [_] So, if you Die, HOW will you become our Elected KING of **"The New RIGHTEOUS One-World Government!"** Book 016? {See www.Amazon.com for: **"The CONSTITUTION for the New RIGHTEOUS One-World Government!" (How all Peoples can get True Justice, and Celebrate the Great Year of JUBILEE!) By The Worldwide People's Revolution!® Book 016B.}** †

08-19 [_] Well, I will have to be Resurrected from the Dead, at the Time when I am Needed for that Work, which will be called *"a Great Work and a Marvelous Wonder,"* when almost all of the Leaders of all Nations will be brought to Court in the Vatican Building, in Saint Peter's Basilica, in Rome: beCause it is Designed Perfectly for such a Great Meeting of the Most-Intelligent and Well-Educated Minds, in the Form of a CROSS, whereby the People who Agree with me will Sit at my Right-hand Side, and the People who Disagree with me will Sit at my Left-hand Side, and the News Reporters, Doubters, Skeptics, and Masses of People will be Seated in the Leg or Nave of the Cross and also Congregate in the Plaza or Forum, Outside, where they can Watch the Trial by Wide Flat-screen TVs, which will be Set Up in all Streets, Worldwide, so that all Peoples might Gather to Watch it, and Devote their Full Attention to it, if they do not have Good TVs at Home, or in their Churches, Schools, Court Houses, Ball Parks, Gymnasiums, Theaters, Concert Halls, Prisons, Hospitals, or wherever. Yes, it is called: **"The GREAT Worldwide TELEVISED Court HEARING!" (That Great Meeting of the Most Intelligent and Well-Educated Minds!) By The Worldwide People's Revolution!® Book 041B.** †‡

08-20 [_] I will have to Confess one Thing, O Elected King, and that is the Fact that you have a Great Imagination! Yes, you Think on a Grand Scale, like no other Person who ever Lived! Are you Sure that you are not the Reincarnation of Jesus Christ, himself? †‡

08-21 [_] I am Positively Sure that I am NOT, and neither is anyone else: beCause Jesus is now Immortal and Living in Mount Zion, which is the Holy City of the Great King.

08-22 [_] So, when is he going to Return to Jerusalem, in order to Establish his Righteous One-World Government over all of the Nations?

08-23 [_] Well, he cannot Return, until we Build the Great World TEMPLE of PEACE. {See www.Amazon.com for: **"The Great World TEMPLE of PEACE!" (The Glory of Jerusalem Arises Again in the Great State of Flexible Texas!) By The Worldwide People's Revolution!® Book 017B.**}

08-24 [_] So, how long will that Require?

08-25 [_] Well, if we get to Work on it, right away, I would say about 6 Years. Moreover, during that same Time, we need to Construct no less than 100,000 Beautiful Planned City States. † {See the above Website for: **"The Right Design for Living!" (A List of Great Advantages for Building Beautiful Planned City States!) By The Worldwide People's Revolution!®** Book 012B.}

08-26 [_] So, it looks like we have our Work "Cut Out" for us, right?

08-27 [_] Well, my Friend, some People have been Incessantly Complaining for several Years about Unemployment, Underemployment, and Low Wages. Therefore, it is now Time for them to Join: **"The Swanky Associations of Working Soldiers!" (A Fascinating Collection of Various Kinds of Voluntary Working Soldiers!) By The Worldwide People's Revolution!®** Book 018B. Indeed, they can Earn as much as 120$ per Hour for Extremely Hard Skilled Labor during the Heat or Cold, and Retire after just 6 Years of Common Skilled Labor, or the Equivalent thereof — such as Setting Marble Tiles on the Solid Stone Walls of their own Stone Dome Home Complexes — without any Loans, without any Interest, and without any Taxes: beCause they will not have to OWN any such Expensive Houses; but, they will get to Live in them, until they Die, even as the President Livz in the White House, in Washington, District of Chief Criminals! However, if they Want to Own such Expensive "Beautiful Swanky Stone Dome Home COMPLEXES!" (HOW to Build SECURE Tax-proof, Insurance-proof, Self-air-conditioned, Paint-proof, Rot-proof, Termite-proof, Mouse-proof, Fireproof, Tornado-proof, Hurricane-proof, Thief-proof, and BOMB-PROOF Houses!) By The

Worldwide People's Revolution!® Book 102, they are also Welcome to make Slaves of themselves for doing that, at Cost, and it will not Bother me the Slightest Bit: beCause I will get to Liv in **"The Great World TEMPLE of PEACE!"** in **"A New Jerusalem in the Great State of Flexible Texas!" (HOW to make Good Use of the Mississippi River!) By The Worldwide People's Revolution!®** Book 090. †‡

08-28 [_] That Sounds too Good to be True. Therefore, I do not Believe that it is Possible.

08-29 [_] Well, that is only beCause you have not yet Studied my Master Plan, which Explains it in Undeniable Details, which can be Proven in a Courtroom. ‡

08-30 [_] So, are you Willing to BET on it?

08-31 [_] Absolutely! In Fact, if you can Prove in a Courtroom that my Master Plan is Unworkable, or even Unreasonable, you may Claim all of my Property. Guaranteed. ‡

08-32 [_] So, just how much Property do you Possess?

08-33 [_] Well, when you consider the Value of my Multitude of Inspired Books, I would say that I Possess a Considerable Amount of Valuable Property — well into the Billions of Dollars-worth. Moreover, anyone on the Earth presently has my Permission to Sell any of my Inspired Books, and keep 90% of the Net Profits: beCause I only want 10% of the Net Profits for the Construction of **the Great World TEMPLE of PEACE**, in that New Jerusalem!

08-34 [_] Well, that certainly sounds rather Generous of you, O Selected King. However, it seems like it should be the other Way around, whereby we keep the 10 percent, while you get the 90 percent of the Net Profits: beCause you did all of the Work to Write the Books, while we did none of it. Indeed, that is how most People would handle it, if they Self-published the Books. However, if they went through a normal Edomite Publisher, he or she would get 90% of the Net Profits, and Laugh all of the way to the Bank, which is what you are now Inviting all of those Lying Edomites to DO! So, does that not Bother you? ‡

08-35 [_] ♦♦♦♦ Well, unlike Edomite Capitalists, I am not a Selfish Person. After all, it was very little Effort for me to Write my Inspired Books, which just Flowed Out of me like a River of Water. For Example, this Book has taken me all of Parts of 2 Days, up to this Point, just to write about 30,855 words, which I Challenge anyone else on this Earth to do, seeing that this one little Book will put Medical Snakes OUT of Business, while Paving the Way for True Health Care, which will Save the People of the World no less than Millions of Trillions of Dollars during the next few hundred Years! †§‡

08-36 [_] Are you kidding!? — This book will have no more effect on the medical industry than a mouse would have eating on a silo full of a million tons of wheat. †‡

08-37 [_] And how much Money are you Willing to Bet on that? Remember the True-Life Story about the Old Black Mare, called LUCY, which you can find in Chapters 03—04, which can be and will be Proven in a Courtroom, if I get my Way!

08-38 [_] Well, I would not be so Stupid as to Bet on it, O Selected King: beCause I might Lose the Bet: beCause your other Inspired Books might be more Powerful and Popular than this one. After all, I have not Studied your other Books. †‡ {Try: **"The Low Court of Supreme Injustices is Brought to Trial!" (Our Elected King Butts Heads with the United States Supreme Court, with or without their Black Robes of Hypocrisies and Lies!)**, Book 011B, plus: **"The UGLY Scarred Dishonest Face of Poor Old Miserable UNCLE SAM!" (A Memorial Day Legacy!)**, Book 054, plus: **"Our Elected King Who Speaks Out!" (It is High Time for some Sane Person to Get Control of this Insane World!) By The Worldwide People's Revolution!®** Book 070, which is a Companion Book of: "Our Selected King SPEAKS OUT!" (It is High Time for some Sane Person to get Total Control of this Insane World!) By The Worldwide People's Revolution!® Book 100! Yes, it is a Companion Book of: "The CONDENSED Version of MARK TWAIN Races for the PRESIDENCY with a Landslide VICTORY!" (The 2020 Presidential Candidates Desperately Need Some STRONG Undefeatable COMPETITION!) By The Worldwide People's Revolution!® Book 033C.}

08-39 [_] Awe, I see that you are Wiser than most People. Therefore, being a Wise Person, how about Experimenting with my Books? Yes, how about Selling them for a Reasonable Price, just to Discover how Well they Sell, in spite of all of the Capitalized Words? Yes, just get yourself 2 or 3 Copies of each of 40 Books, and set up a Public Display of them on a Sheet of Plywood, which rests on a 2-feet-high Stand, which has 10 books wide and 4 high, on a very Busy Street Corner, where

People can See them; and then raise your Right Hand, pointing toward the Books, and Shout Out these Words: "**These are the Inspired Books of just one Blest Author, who Wrote all of these Books in just 2 Years of Time, which are Guaranteed to Satisfy the Belly of your Mind!**" And then, be Prepared to quickly run out of Books to Sell: beCause Potential Intelligent Customers will Naturally take a Look Inside of them, and read a Sentence or 2, by Chance, and be Struck Dead-center in their Thinking Cavity with some Provable Truths, which will Grab their Attention, you might say, and Arouse their Curiosity to the Point of Wanting at least one Book to Examine from Cover to Cover, which may very well be this Book, or: "**Poverty Hunger Riots Strikes Police Brutalities Election Deceptions and Civil Wars!**" (The High Price that we Earthlings have Paid for Leaving the Good Land!) By The Worldwide People's Revolution!® Book 014B. Otherwise, they might Discover a really HOT Book, called: "**GOOD NEWS for REBEL WOMEN!**" (How almost all Wives can become Moderately RICH without Leaving their Homes! Guaranteed!) By The Worldwide People's Revolution!® Book 010. However, I Prefer: "Good Lessons for Honest Wise Men!" (A Simplistic Plan for Totally Solving the Complicated Problems of Deceived Mankind!) **By** The Smarter Professor of Common Sense! Book 125. †

08-40 [_] So, you have an Incredible Amount of Confidence in your own Abilities, huh? Is that not called VANITY? †

— Chapter 09 —

How to Treat the Mentally Sick People

09-01 [_] O Selected King, you should seriously consider going to some Psychopath Medical Doctor, and seek a Treatment for your own Mental Illness: beCause there is no Way in this World that the Medical Establishment and Drug Industries can be put OUT of Business — not even if half of the Population of the World Agrees with you: beCause the other half is Totally Addicted to their Drugs, and would not know HOW to Live without them. †‡ {See: "HOW to Become a HOLY Man!" (40 Good Reasons WHY People Should FAST and PRAY!) By The Worldwide People's Revolution!® Book 045.}

09-02 [_] You are Forgetting a Major Element in your Mixture of Horrible Thoughts. What if the Rain should STOP, and there is nothing to Eat nor Drink — how Long will it be before the Masses of People

Wake Up and come to their Right Senses with the Prodigal Son in *Luke 15*? {See: *"What will you Do when the Rain STOPS?"* (God's Last Resort to Save Mankind from his MADNESS!) By The Worldwide People's Revolution!® Book 101, *"The New MAGNIFIED Version of The GOOD NEWS According to Saint LUKE!"* (The Magnified Gospel of Saint Luke in Plain English!) By The Worldwide People's Revolution!® Book 061, plus: *"The Gospel According to our Elected King!"* (The Good News from the Most Modern Perspective!) By The Worldwide People's Revolution!® Book 077.}

09-03 [_] Hmmm, that is a Factor that I did not Calculate in my Thinking. Perhaps you are Right — an Empty Stomach might Cause them to THINK and even Remember the Good Old Days! However, that does not Mean that all such People are going to take up Reading Insane Books, like this one. †§‡

09-04 [_] Well, if this Book is so "Insane," WHY are you now Reading it?

09-05 [_] You got me Penned Down on that one, O Elected King. So, how am I going to Cover my Shame?

09-06 [_] Well, the Best Way to Cover your Shame is to Sell Copies of this Book to other People, even if they do not normally like to Read: beCause most books are just Trash; but, none of my Inspired Books can be Classified as Trash: beCause, like the *Bible,* they contain Long-enduring Provable Truths. Indeed, the more that one Thinks about all such Great Truths, the more one is Persuaded that all such Words should be "Re-red," and perhaps a dozen Times or more, just to Absorb the Richness of them, and especially: **"LIGHTNING STRIKES Versus Lightning Bugs!" (How you can Become Moderately RICH, without Telling any Lies nor Selling any Trash!) By The Worldwide People's Revolution!®** Book 074. Yes, that is the Best of Fine Literature in these Times, which should be Mandatory Reading in all Public Schools, Worldwide. ‡

09-07 [_] So, do you Believe that that can be Proven in a Courtroom with Law and Order? If so, why do we Lawyers not bring you to Court to Prove it, and perhaps Lock you up in a Nut House for being INSANE? After all, that Book is so full of Sarcasms, and God knows what else, so that not even William Shakingspears could handle it. ‡§

09-08 [_] Well, that Good Book only seems to be Insane to you: beCAUSE of your Ignorance, even as Medical Science seems to be Insane to me: beCAUSE of my Ignorance. After all, it is not Possible that Millions of Medical Doctors could be WRong about the Workings of the Human Body and Mind, while I and a few others, alone, are Riit about it! †§‡

09-09 [_] Trust me, you are WRong about them: beCause Medical Doctors are as Necessary as Lawyers, Judges, Policemen, Prisons, and Politicians. ‡§

09-10 [_] I See that you have not Studied: **"The Low Court of Supreme Injustices is Brought to Trail!" (Our Elected King Butts Heads with the United States Supreme Court, with or without their Black Robes of Hypocrisies and Lies!) By The Worldwide People's Revolution!®** Book 011B, much less: "The Sixth Book of Moses called GOOD GOVERNMENT!" (The Primary Missing Book in the Holy Bible!) **By** The Worldwide People's Revolution!® Book 126.

09-11 [_] I would say that she Failed to Study: **"The PRAYERS of PUMPKINHEADS!" (Even God Needs a Little Humor to Cheer himself Up!),** Book 007, as well as: **"The Washington Journal is a FARCE!" (C-SPAN Managers are not very WISE!) By The Worldwide People's Revolution!®** Book 006. Yes, I would say that she is Suffering with Chronic Constipation of the Mind!

09-12 [_] I would say that she will come to her Riit Sensuz when the Rain STOPS. {See www.Amazon.com for: "How Best to Prepare for CLIMATE CHANGES!" (The Wisest Plan for Mankind to Follow!) By The Worldwide People's Revolution!® Book 004B.

09-13 [_] I would say that she should Study: **"WHY do I have to be Surrounded by CRAZY PEOPLE?" (Do almost all People Feel like they are Surrounded by Crazy People??) By The Worldwide People's Revolution!®** Book 005B.

09-14 [_] I would say that she completely Overlooked one of the Best Books in the World, called: "What is WRong with those Professing Christians?" (A Self-Examination of the Heart of the Body of Good Government!) By The Worldwide People's Revolution!® Book 002B.

09-15 [_] God have Mercy! — by the Time she finishes Reading all of those Inspired Books with a Capital R, she will be Insane for Sure! That is, unless she is Converted from her Evil Ways! And there is that Slight Possibility! Yes, I have already Changed my Mind about the Goodness of DRUGS, which most People Lived Well without for thousands of Years! †§‡

09-16 [_] Awe, I see that you do not have your Facts very Straight. People did NOT Live WELL for thousands of Years without Drugs. In Fact, the Average Lifespan, just 200 Years Ago, was only 25: beCause half of the Babies DIED before they were 2! Moreover, if they did not Die as little Children, half of those who Lived passed 2 just Happened to Die before they were 12: beCause of the Love of GOD, who Invented all of those Good Sicknesses and Wonderful Diseases! Moreover, as if that were not Bad enough, the ones who Lived through all such Sicknesses and Diseases often Died in Unnecessary Wars and Accidents, if they were Men, which Naturally Lowered the Life Expectancy of MEN. Therefore, we can Thank Satan for those Drugs: beCause we now Live to an Average of 75 Years. †§‡

09-17 [_] Perhaps it was the Drugs that Killed most of those Babies 200 Years Ago: beCause they had some really Weird Beliefs back in those Days. In Fact, President George Washington Died from having too much of his Blood let out, which was a Common "Cure" for anything from Headaches to Measles and Mumps. †§‡

09-18 [_] They only needed to Stop Drinking Cow's Milk and Eating Cheese, and none of them would have had any Measles nor Mumps, let along Whooping Cough and Strep Throat or Tonsillitis. After all, none of the Wild Apes Suffer with any such Diseases. †§‡

09-19 [_] How come Father Abraham did not have such Diseases, since he was a Meat-eating Milk-drinking Cheese-a-holic and Workaholic? †§‡ (See *Genesis 18.*)

09-20 [_] Father Abraham Lived for 175 Years, and Isaac Lived 180 Years, while Jacob Lived for only 160 Years, and his Son Joseph Lived for only 110 Years: beCause of the Stress of Living in Egypt. However, Adam Lived for 930 Years, and Methuselah 966 Years, and never had a Sick Day during his entire Life! †‡

09-21 [_] I do not Believe any of those Exaggerated Jewish Fairy Tales; but, I do Know for a Fact that my Great Great Grandparents did not Die at the Young Age of 25. In Fact, if most People Lived until they were Adults, most of them Lived until they were 70 to 100 or more, and without any MediSINZ: beCause they were a lot Stronger and Healthier back then, than People are Today: beCause they did not have all of the Harmful Chemicals and Poisons to Deal with. Furthermore, this Younger Generation has a long ways to go, just to Catch Up with them, and might not Live half as Long: beCause of Eating those Junk Foods. †‡

09-22 [_] Well, that is Debatable. Nevertheless, I have never seen so many Sickly nor Insane Children, who Suffer with thousands of Ailments that People did not used to have. So, how do you Account for that?

09-23 [_] What this World needs is another Kind of Black Plague, which Wipes Out 90% of the Population: beCause this World is far too Overpopulated; and the Best Way to do that is Shoot Shots of Pus into their Butts, whereby their Bodies have no Natural Immunities to anything. Yes, many Great and Fair Cities of Confusion could be left without an Inhabitant: beCause of the Seven Last Great Plagues! (Read *the Book of Revelation*.) †§‡ (See *Jeremiah 4:7; 9:11; 26:9; 34:22; 44:22; 46:19; 51:29, and 37.*)

09-24 [_] One Thing is for Certain — if we do not Change our Ways of Living, we are all going to end up in Self-made Insane Asylums: beCause of Demanding more of our Minds and Bodies than they can Tolerate. Yes, the STRESS will Kill us: beCause Human Beings were not Designed for it; but, they were Designed for the *Garden of Eden,* who was the Holy Angel who Set Up the Garden for Adam and Eve. †‡

09-25 [_] I am more Worried about Survival. Indeed, the Islamic Terrorists are liable to Kill ALL of us, if the Medical Doctors do not get around to it, first. In Fact, more than 800,000 Americans Die each Year from Bad Medical Practices, who may be Setting their own Trap with their Hateful Shots of Pus and Countless Pills and Endless Doctor Bills, which Cause more Stress on all such Poor People, who cannot Afford to Pay any such Bills, which none of them should have had, to begin with. After all, the Public Schools could Teach to the Children what is Best for them to Eat, so as to Avoid all such Sicknesses and Diseases; but, they Sorely Lack any Confidence in *Genesis 1:29.* †§‡

09-26 [_] I have no Idea what *Genesis 1:29* is all about. Moreover, I am not going to read that Unholy Mutilated Bible, even if it Kills me:

beCause it has Driven many People INSANE, who have no Idea HOW to be Saved from it. †§‡

09-27 [_] Well, my Friend, all Cases of Insanity are easy to Cure by simply FASTING and PRAYING. Yes, you can Prove it by Doing it. †‡

09-28 [_] Is that for Real? If so, why does the President not Try it? After all, he says that he will Do this or that, and come next Week, he does just the Opposite! Is that not Insanity? †§‡

09-29 [_] Well, that is not beCause of Insanity; but, beCause the Bankers who Control him have Reversed his Orders, and thus made a Fool of him. Moreover, he must Cooperate with them, or else go down in History as a Complete Failure, which no Proud President would ever Want to do. Therefore, they just Cooperate with those Edomite Zionist Banksters, who are the Puppet Masters, who Handle the Strings on their Political Puppets. †§‡

09-30 [_] So, if someone is Actually Insane, enough Fasting will Cure him or her, huh?

— Chapter 10 —

Medical Remedies Exposed

10-01 [_] The Number One Remedy for almost every Ailment is TIME: beCause, given Enough Time, and a Body can Heal itself from almost any Ailment. Yes, REST and Time was the Ancient Greek Remedy, who had "Sleep Temples," where any Sick, Diseased, Weak, or Wounded People could go to and SLEEP: beCause that is Nature's Cure, even for Insanity, if a Person Persists with it, and just SLEEPS, without Eating nor Drinking anything! †‡

10-02 [_] So, O Doctor Good Health, if that is the Natural Cure for most Ailments, why do Medical Doctors not have Modern "Sleep Temples" for their Patients? Otherwise, why do they not tell their Patients to just stay at Home and SLEEP, until they Recover from whatever Ails them?

10-03 [_] Well, my Friend, how Profitable would that be for Witchdoctors? After all, their Main Objective is to Obtain more MONEY, even though many of them Deny it: beCause everyone Needs LOTS of Money, just to Live, without Living like Kings nor Queens in "Beautiful Swanky PALACES!" (A New Concept in Living Habits — Swanky Palaces for Poor People!) By The Worldwide People's Revolution!® Book 066, which is a Subject that none of them ever Heard of: beCause, it is not Tawt in "The Public School of IGNERUNT FQLZ!" (HOW we have been GRAATLEE DISEEVD by Capitalism!) By The Worldwide People's Revolution!® Book 024B: beCause, that would not be very Profitable for the Slave Masters; nor is it Mentioned by the Snooze Reporters during Evening News Broadcasts: beCause, none of those Edomite Puppets are Looking for "Guaranteed Solutions!" (HOW to Solve our Local and Global Problems in the Most-Rational Manner Possible!) By The Worldwide People's Revolution!® Book 080, for anything: beCause, they do not Want to put themselves Out of Business by Teaching too many Provable Truths: beCause, that would not be very Profitable, which would be like the Fire DEPARTment going all about Town, Teaching the Children how to Build those "Beautiful Swanky Stone Dome Home COMPLEXES!" (HOW to Build SECURE Tax-proof, Insurance-proof, Self-air-conditioned, Paint-proof, Rot-proof, Termite-proof, Mouse-proof, Fireproof, Tornado-proof, Hurricane-proof, Thief-proof, and BOMB-PROOF Houses!) By The Worldwide People's Revolution!® Book 102, which would be like Judges going around Town, Teaching the Children to Learn, Believe, Love, and OBEY **"The New MAGNIFIED Version of the 20 Commandments,"** which can be Found in "LIGHTNING STRIKES Versus Lightning Bugs!" (HOW you can Become Moderately RICH, without Telling any Lies nor Selling any Trash!) By The Worldwide People's Revolution!® Book 074, which might put Judges and Lawyers OUT of Business, as well as Politicians, who just LOVE those Taxes. Moreover, if People just Stayed at Home, and Slept, they would Lose their Jobs, which would not be very Profitable for them. Therefore, as Capitalist Prostitutes, they MUST get back to Work. †‡

10-04 [_] So, O Selected King, are you Suggesting that Medical Doctors are not Near Relatives of Jesus Christ, who have come to SAVE us from our Dietary Sins? Indeed, I have always had it in my Mind that Medical Doctors are the GOOD People, even if they Charge a thousand Dollars per Minute for their Hard Labor, while some Stone Mason might get only 20$ per Hour, if he is located in the right place. Otherwise, he might get 25 Cents per Hour, and only if he Works HARD: beCause there are a hundred other Bodies to take his Place in the Unemployment Line: beCause that is how Capitalism Works, and forever in Favor of the Rich Hogs. However, if Sleeping will Cure us from whatever Ails us, it is Time to REVOLT by going to Sleep. However, WHO would Earn the Money to Pay the Endless Bills, if we all Moved to a Farm, and took up Gardening? †§‡

10-05 [_] ♦♦ And, pray tell, WHY would you have any Endless Bills, if you Lived on a Farm with a dozen other Families, who are Contented to Live a Good Life without any of those Bills, except maybe Property Taxes? Yes, People Lived like that for thousands of Years, and so can we; but, only by United Effort, whereby half of those dozen Families Earns the Money to Support the other half, who Work on the Farm, getting it Prepared for Real Living, having a large Ice House for Cool Drinks during the Summer, and for Refrigeration the Year around; having Stone Walls 10 feet THICK, so as to not have any Heating nor Cooling Bills; having LUSCIOUS All-Mineral Organic Gardens with Stone Walls around them, so that Wild Varmints are not Eating your Fruits; and having Fireproof Stone Dome Home Complexes, which are Designed for True Prosperity, even as I have Explained in other Good Books. {See www.Amazon.com for: "The LUSCIOUS All-Mineral Organic Method of Gardening!" (HOW to Grow DELICIOUS Satisfying Foods for Potential Kingz and Kweenz in Beautiful Swanky PALACES!) By The Worldwide People's Revolution!® Book 021B, "Profitable Swanky MULCHING ROCKS!" (30

Advantages for Using Swanky Mulching Rocks in an All-Mineral Organic Garden!) By The Worldwide People's Revolution!® Book 098, which is a Companion Book of: "Orgimmick Gardening at its Best!" (HOW to Grow Delicious Satisfying Foods without a 10 Million-Dollar Investment!) By The Worldwide People's Revolution!® Book 079, which is a Companion Book of: "Beautiful Swanky Stone Dome Home COMPLEXES!" (HOW to Build SECURE Tax-proof, Insurance-proof, Self-air-conditioned, Paint-proof, Rot-proof, Termite-proof, Mouse-proof, Fireproof, Tornado-proof, Hurricane-proof, Thief-proof, and BOMB-PROOF Houses!) By The Worldwide People's Revolution!® Book 102, "Poverty Hunger Riots Strikes Police Brutalities Election Deceptions and Civil Wars!" (The High Price that we Earthlings have Paid for Leaving the Good Land!) By The Worldwide People's Revolution!® Book 014B, plus: "Seven Great Armies of Working Soldiers!" (HOW to Provide a Way for Everyone to WORK: so as to Eliminate Poverty, Crimes, Drug Abuses, Prisons and Unnecessary Taxes!) By The Worldwide People's Revolution!® Book 015B, which is a Companion Book of: "Terrorists Beware that your Days are Numbered!" (HOW to Bring those Terrorist Attacks to a Screeching HALT!) By The Worldwide People's Revolution!® Book 043, which is a Companion Book of: "Does a Good Soldier have to be a MURDERER?" (Seven Great Swanky Armies of Voluntary Working Soldiers!) By The Worldwide People's Revolution!® Book 027B, which is a Companion Book of: "The Swanky Associations of Working Soldiers!" (A Fascinating Collection of Various Kinds of Voluntary Working Soldiers!) By The Worldwide People's Revolution!® Book 018B, which is a Companion Book of: "God Speaks and the Whole World Listens!" (Fire on the Mountain from the Burning Bush by the Spirit of Truths!) By The Worldwide People's Revolution!® Book 026B, which, of course, no one Wants to REED: beCause none of those Exceptionally Good Books were ever Advertised on the Devil's Vision, called a TV: beCause, it is not Permitted: beCause those Inspired Books are a Great THREAT to the Evil Empire: beCause, the SLAVES might Discover that they could be Eating at those "Royal Swanky Buffets!" (The Best Feasts in the Whole World!) By The Worldwide People's Revolution!® Book 103, for FREE: beCause, X-number of Young Men will be Happy to VOLUNTEER to Provide all of those Good Wholesome Natural Foods for the FUN of it: beCause, in Exchange for 4 Hours of Common Skilled Labor per Workday, they will get to Liv in those "Beautiful Swanky PALACES!" (A New Concept in Living Habits — Swanky Palaces for Poor People!) By The Worldwide People's Revolution!® Book

066! In Fact, there will be BILLIONS of other Poor Education Slaves, who will be Happy to Help those Unemployed Work Slaves to Build those **"GLORIOUS Swanky Hotels Castles and Fortresses!"** (Beautiful Planned City States for WISE Intelligent Well-Educated People with Common Sense and Good Understanding!) By The Worldwide People's Revolution!® Book 019B, whereby they might Raise their Standards of Living by at least 100 Times: beCause we now have Mechanical Slaves, which can do the Work of TRILLIONS of People, for FREE! For Example, instead of Wasting Money on an Expensive Army Tank, that Money can be Spent Wisely on 100 Swanky Rock-cutting Machines and Rock-polishing Machines! But, you have never Heard that Good News on the Evening Snooze Reports: beCause those Edomite Slave Masters would not Like it! In Fact, they would be Mocking all such Good Ideas, and calling it COMMUNISM! §‡}

10-06 |_| Hmmm, I have never Thought about Moving to some Little Farm: beCause I have always thought of it as being very Boring and far too much Work without any Pay; but, by United Effort, I suppose that a dozen Families could possibly make it Work, if they were Determined to do so. First of all, they would need to have the same Religion, and Agree to Block Out all other Religions, lest they should get into Biblical Arguments of Biblical Proportions. For Example, if one Family did not Accept the Virgin Birth of Jesus Christ Doctrine, the other Families would be ready to Murder them for their Unbelief, just like ISIS (Israeli Secret Instigation Services) wants to get Rid of all Unbelievers in Buzzeldick the Great: beCause, like it or not, none of those False Religions have been Proven to be False, at: **"The GREAT Worldwide TELEVISED Court HEARING!"** (That Great Meeting of the Most-Intelligent and Well-Educated Minds!) By The Worldwide People's Revolution!® Book 041B, whereby all such False Religions might be Debunked within Minutes, by **"The Swanky Sword of Divine Truths!"** (The Most-Powerful Weapon in the Whole Universe!) By The Worldwide People's Revolution!® Book 067. Yes, it would be like that False Accusation about me Proposing a New Form of COMMUNISM, which I will now Debunk in one Short Sentence, my Friend. So, Reed it Carefully and Prayerfully: beCause, you cannot Defeat the Sharp Sword of Provable Truths! Neither Capitalism, Socialism, Fascism, nor Communism ever Proposed to get everyone Set Up PROPERLY on the Land to Feed and Clothe themselves with True SECURITY, within the Borders of those **"GLORIOUS Swanky Hotels Castles and Fortresses!"** (Beautiful Planned City States for WISE Intelligent Well-Educated People with Common Sense and Good Understanding!) By The Worldwide People's Revolution!® Book

019B: beCAUSE, until NOW, it was Impossible to Do that: beCause Mankind did not have the Technologies to Do it, much less, the FAITH, Hope, Trust, Love, Patience, Persistence, nor OBEDIENCE: beCause of Visualizing what is Required for getting everyone Set Up PROPERLY for LIVING, and Working at HOME! Indeed, they never Heard of: "The New RIGHTEOUS One-World Government!" (HOW to Establish a Righteous One-World Government without Going to WAR!) By The Worldwide People's Revolution!® Book 056, until NOW: beCause, that would also be a Great THREAT to the Evil Empire! †§‡§§

10-07 |_| ♦♦♦ Well, my Friend, it does Pay to have the same Religious Beliefs; but, you can Greatly Simplify your Beliefs by just Accepting MY Beliefs, whereby all Religious Arguments will be Dissolved: beCause no one can Fight Against "The Swanky Sword of Divine Truths!" and Win. Therefore, if you can Discover other Readers of my Inspired Books, you will likely Discover the Right People to Live with — that is, IF they have Filled Out and Filed "The Complete SURVEYS of our VALUES!" (SURVEYS of Religious Spiritual Political Governmental Sexual Social Moral Economical Business Labor Habitual and Miscellaneous VALUES!) By The Worldwide People's Revolution!® Book 059, which is a Companion Book of: "The Simplistic SURVEYS of our VALUES!" Book 059B, which even a DUNCE could figure out. For Example, do you Sincerely Want to Liv with THIEVES, Liars, and ROBBERS? |_| NO, of course NOT! Therefore, just Check the Appropriate Boxes, my Friend, and the Computers will Discover your Check Marks, and get you Lined Up with other People of Like-mindedness, whereby you can Liv in Perfect PEACE: beCause you all Agree to NOT Steal, Lie, Rob, nor CHEAT yourselves: beCause, you have no Desires to make yourselves Miserable, and have to TAX yourselves to Pay Needless Property Taxes, nor Hire Policemen to Guard each other, when you can Guard yourselves with Perfect PEACE: beCause, if you Discover some Criminal, all that you have to Do is to BANISH him or her from your Peaceful Swanky Fortress, and that Problem will be over with! §‡

10-08 |_| Well, O Selected King, I suppose that I could try Selling your Books on the Streets, if the Police did not quickly Arrest me for it: beCause of Discovering such Controversial Books as this one; and that Way I might Discover some Like-minded People, who would Naturally be coming back to Buy more Books, or Different Books — such as: "GOOD NEWS for REBEL WOMEN!" (HOW almost all Wives can become Moderately RICH without Leaving their Homes! Guaranteed!) By The Worldwide People's Revolution!® Book 010B, plus: "Are you a Jobless Graduate of the SKQL uv FQLZ?" (HOW to Get a GOUD EJUKAASHUN without Robbing the Bank!) By The Worldwide People's Revolution!® Book 020B. Yes, I could Guarantee those Books to Satisfy them, and offer a Money-back Guarantee, if they are not Perfectly Satisfied with them, if the Books are just returned in Good Conditions. However, who in their Riit Mind would Return a Collector's Item, which might be Worth a Million Dollars during the Future, such as: "The Sixth Book of Moses called GOOD GOVERNMENT!" (The Primary Missing Book in the Holy Bible!) By The Worldwide People's Revolution!® Book 126? †§‡§§

10-09 [_] Well, my Friend, you will never know the Results of it, if you never Test it. I would say that it would all Depend on WHERE you are Located, and how Friendly and Honest you are. Indeed, some of the Books might Sell like Hotdogs in the Right Places. You might Test this one near some Hospital; but, not where they can Arrest you for "Disturbing the Peace," or some other Silly Excuse. Indeed, you could even Offer this Book to them for Free, if they will Promise to Return it to you if they do not Like it, or Pay for it, if they do Like it, even though, being Sons and Daughters of Capitalism, you would likely never See them again: beCause their Promises are about as Good as those of Judas Iscariot and Burn-me MADoff. Nevertheless, it will not be a Waste of your Money, if they Actually read the Book: beCause, whomever Rejects the Great Truths that I have Revealed within this Inspired Book will be CURSED! Yes, I now put a Curse on all such Rejecters of Truths, and Pray that God will Humble them to the Dust, if they do not REPENT! Therefore, if they do not Keep their Promises to Return the Books, or else Pay for them, they will be Cursed for it; and you may Check up on them in the Obituaries and Mortuaries: beCause they Deserve the Seven Last Great Plagues! Yes, I am the Man with the Spirit of Elijah, O Fools! †§‡

10-10 [_] That Sounds rather Frightening, O Elected King. Suppose they are Unable to Return the Books, or otherwise not Pay for them — will they still be Cursed with Sicknesses, Diseases, Plagues, Accidents, Wars, and DEATHS?

10-11 [_] ♦ Well, I Pray to God that they will be Cursed, if they do not Keep their Promises. After all, they can always Ask someone else to Return the Books for them, and even get their Money back, if they are not Satisfied, which no one could ever do at a Restaurant, after Eating the entire Meal! Therefore, if they are not Sure that they Want the Book, they should read a Chapter or 2 while standing on the Street, or in your

Book Store. After all, the Information within this one Book could Save them tens of thousands of Dollars, and could even Save their Lives. Therefore, it is a Small Price to Pay for such Valuable Information, which could be Sold for 10 Times the Price, and it would still be Perfectly Fair. After all, a Medical Doctor thinks nothing of Charging a thousand dollars for 10 Minutes of Work. Likewise, a Politician thinks nothing of Selling a single Dinner at a Political Rally for a thousand dollars. Indeed, they have Offered such Meals to me; but, I have always turned them down: beCause I Know for a Fact that they are not at all Interested in anything that I might have to Teach to them. So, their "Friendship" is just a Charade, while my Friendship is for REAL, which you can Discover in: "Are Americans the Most-STUPID People who ever Lived?" (HOW Working People can PROSPER and Live in PEACE Under the Rulership of a RIGHTEOUS KING!) By The Worldwide People's Revolution!® Book 047, which is a Companion Book of: "HOW Righteousness can Overcome Wickedness!" (The Triumph of the Soul who Knows God!) By The Enlightened Professor of Common Sense! Book 093, which is a Companion Book of: "All of the Arguments are in Favor of our Selected King, who has Zero Challengers!" (Before you Attend another Election Deception, you should Carefully Study this Inspired Book with an Honest Open Mind!) By The Worldwide People's Revolution!® Book 085, which is a Companion Book of: "VOTE for The GOAT!" (The New Political Party that has Guaranteed Solutions for our Massive Problems!) By The Worldwide People's Revolution!® Book 109, which is a Companion Book of: "MARK TWAIN Races for the PRESIDENCY with a Landslide VICTORY!" (The 2020 Presidential Candidates Desperately Need Some STRONG Undefeatable COMPETITION!) By The Worldwide People's Revolution!® Book 033B, which is a Companion Book of: "The CONDENSED Version of MARK TWAIN Races for the PRESIDENCY with a Landslide VICTORY!" (The 2020 Presidential Candidates Desperately Need Some STRONG Undefeatable COMPETITION!) By The Worldwide People's Revolution!® Book 033C. †§‡

10-12 [_] So, O Selected King, maybe the Best Way to Sell such Books as this, is to Stand in front of the Hospital with a Box of them for Sale, huh? After all, they would certainly get the Attention of almost all Medical Doctors, who could not Deny the Provable Truths within this Book, without being CURSED for it! †‡

10-13 [_] Well, I Pronounce a DOUBLE Curse on them, if they Reject the Provable Truths within this Inspired Book: beCause they have

Firsthand Knowledge concerning the Human Body, and Know for a FACT that the Internal Uncleanness of Mankind is the Source of all Sicknesses and Diseases, just as Jesus Taught. (See *Matthew 23*.) †‡

10-14 [_] So, O Selected King, will all such Information not become a Great THREAT to their Evil Empire? Indeed, will they not be Seeking to Assassinate YOU, O Elected King of **"The United States of the Whole World!" (A True Global Economy for the Masses of Working People!) By The Worldwide People's Revolution!® Book 055?** Will they not get RID of you for Revealing Great Truths that they cannot Prove to be WRong at: **"The GREAT Worldwide TELEVISED Court HEARING!" (That Great Meeting of the Most-Intelligent and Well-Educated Minds!) By The Worldwide People's Revolution!® Book 041B?**

10-15 [_] Well, my Friend, God has Revealed to me that I will be Dead and Gone by then; and therefore, it will be rather Difficult for them to Assassinate me. Therefore, do not Worry about it. Just Concentrate your Time, Money and Energy on "The GWTCH!" Book 041B. †§‡

10-16 [_] So, O Selected King, will they not be Seeking to Assassinate all of us who are Selling all such Books? Will they not be Hiring Thugs to Burn our Book Stores? Moreover, will Amazon dot com not be Threatened by them, and perhaps Murdered by them?

10-17 [_] Well, if they Suffer for Publishing the Truth, they will be Blest for it: beCause I Pronounce a Great Blessing on them for Helping to Publish the Truth concerning any Subject.

10-18 [_] So, what if your Books are Banned from Amazon dot com, how will they get Published?

10-19 [_] Well, anyone in the World has my Permission to Sell my Books for a Profit, if they are Inclined to do so, and also Keep 90% of the Net Profits for themselves: beCause I only want 10% of the Net Profits for Constructing **"The Great World TEMPLE of PEACE!" (The Glory of Jerusalem Arises Again in the Great State of Flexible Texas!) By The Worldwide People's Revolution!® Book 017B,** which will be the Tallest and Largest Building in the whole World! Yes, it will be the HEADQUARTERS for: **"The New RIGHTEOUS One-World Government!" (HOW to Establish a Righteous One-World Government without Going to WAR!) By The Worldwide People's Revolution!® Book 056,** which will Conduct Televised Court Hearings, until all of the Important Issues are Settled, in COURT: beCause, that is the Peaceful Way to do it, which you can Fully Understand, if you Study: **"An Amazing Collection of Wit and Wisdom!" (The Marvelous Tale of the Colorful Peacock from Angel Ridge, and the Strong Rope of Everlasting Hope!) By The Worldwide People's Revolution!® Book 048.** Therefore, take some Time to Study it, my Friend, and do not be left in the Darkness of Ignorance with the Dimwitcrats, Independent Jackasses, nor Reprobates, who Reside in: **"The BIG White OUTHOUSE on the Not-so-Biblical Capitol DUNGHILL!" (The Chief Sins of the Divided States of United Lies!) By The Worldwide People's Revolution!®** Book 023B, which Stinks from the Top to the Bottom with Ancient Elephant Droppings and Fresh Political Donkey Dung!

10-20 [_] So, O Selected King, you have Faith that God will Protect your Books, and get them Published to all Nations, and in all Major Languages, sooner or later, huh?

10-21 [_] Yes, I have Faith in it. After all, why would God Inspire me to Write so many Good Books, if he had no Intentions of Helping me to Publish them? The Truth is that he Works in Strange Ways, since I am probably the Least Qualified to do any Writing for any Cause, being a Grade School DROPOUT, you might say, which is the Truth of it! After all, I could not get along with most of my School Teachers; but, I got along very Well with the Students, whereby only one Student ever Bucked Up Against me, and he Apologized for it, later: beCause, he just needed Time to Think about it, and Talk with his Parents about it, who Assured him that he was Destined to become another one of those **"Modern Deceived SLAVES!" (10 Simple Steps for Liberating ALL Modern Slaves, Worldwide, Including Yourself!) By Liberty and Justice for ALL! Book 113,** even if he got a so-called "good education": beCause the only Truly Free People are those Wild Mountain Goats, who have NO Taxes, who can Leap right over the Heads of those Medical Snakes: beCause they have no Interest in any of their Poisonous Drugs: beCause, they Liv on Natural Wholesome Diets, whereby they do not get Sick nor Diseased, until they come into Contact with PEOPLE, who are the Curse of the Whole Earth! Yes, they are nothing but **"Modern Deceived SLAVES!"** who should Carefully Study: **"The New MAGNIFIED Version of the Book of ACTS!" (The Understandable Version of the Acts of the Apostles in Plain English!) By The Worldwide People's Revolution!®** Book 063: beCause, there are **"Good Lessons for Honest Wise Men!" (A Simplistic Plan for Totally**

Solving the Complicated Problems of Deceived Mankind!) **By The Smarter Professor of Common Sense! Book 125.** †§‡

10-22 [_] But, O Selected King, you have the Assistance of Doctor Samuel Walker Edison, who is very Professional, who is no Grade School DROP OUT — will he not Help you to get it Done?

10-23 [_] Well, my Friend, it will Require tens of thousands of Believers to make it Happen in a BIG Way, as it should. After all, we are talking about putting ALL False Medical Doctors OUT of Business, along with ALL Phony Politicians, Greedy Bankers, Wicked Lawyers, Unjust Judges, Brutal Policemen, Cruel Tax Masters, Lying Scientists, Deceptive Preachers, Drug Pushers, Monsanto, General ElecTrickery, Ford Motors (unless they Change their Ways and begin to Produce Necessary Equipment for Good Working), and all other Enemies of Mankind, even if they must be Cursed with the Seven Last Great Plagues, which the Angels of God can Manage! †§‡§§

10-24 [_] So, O Selected King, a GOOD Medical Doctor would Agree with the Provable Truths within this Inspired Book, and would Help to Publish it, huh? Likewise, the Honest Lawyers would also Agree with those Truths, and therefore Help to Publish such Books, huh? Moreover, Just Judges would Stand Up for all such Truths, and Demand that such Words should be Proven, Riit?

10-25 [_] Yes, my Dear Friend, that is all True — the Good People would Support whatever can be Proven to be GOOD, and anyone with the Faith of a Piss Ant can Prove the Great Benefits of Fasting, by Doing it; but, only IF they Follow **"The Proper RULES for FASTING!"** (The **Complete Instruction Manual for True Repentance!**) **By The Worldwide People's Revolution!®** Book 046. Therefore, do not Try to Cheat: beCause you will only be Cheating yourself, and could even Cause other Innocent People to Stumble over your Deceptions, Lies and Misjudgments. After all, we have our Elected King, himself, for a Good Example of a Holy Man, who can Hear the Voice of God. Otherwise, how could he Write such a Good Book as this within just 3 or 4 Days, and even Proof-read it TWICE? Just Try it yourself, if you Imagine that you are Able to Do such a Thing without the Inspiration of some GOD. Trust me, God is in it. God did it! †‡

10-26 [_] HUMBUG! — anyone with a Working Mind could write a better book than this one, within a day or 2, and especially if such an author had 4 or 5 Sexetaries to get everything correct. †§‡

10-27 [_] Are you Aware that Mark Twain spent 8 Years writing *The Adventures of Huckleberry Finn*, which never sold even one hundredth as many copies as this Inspired Book will Sell? †§‡

10-28 [_] And WHY was that?

10-29 [_] Well, that is beCause nothing in the World can Compete with God's Inspiration, which Speaks with our Hearts and Minds. After all, this Book does not Stand all ALONE: beCause it is Supported by all of the Information within our Elected King's other Inspired Books, which many People Judge to be much Better than this Book — such as: "The New MAGNIFIED Version of the HOLY KORAN!" (WHY MuhamMAD went to Hell for Spiritual MURDER!) By The Worldwide People's Revolution!® Book 089, which is a Masterpiece of Fine Artistic Literature! However, if you were Sick and/or Diseased, and had Faith in the Great Truths within this Good Book, you could be Healed from your Sickness and/or Disease, and then you would Credit this Book with your Salvation from it, whereby it might even become your Favorite Book on the Earth, and Especially if you had been Suffering with Great PAINS, and all of your Pains simply CEASED, after Fasting for just 4 or 5 Days, on nothing but 2 Cups of Spring Water per Day! †§‡

10-30 [_] Is that Actually Possible, O Doctor Samuel Walker Edison?

— Chapter 11 —

Pains are Warning Signs along the Highway of Life

{Just one Good Grape Vine can Produce 14 Tons of Delicious Grapes! But, only IF they are Grown by "The LUSCIOUS All-Mineral Organic Method of Gardening!" (HOW to Grow DELICIOUS Satisfying Foods for Potential Kingz and Kweenz in Beautiful Swanky PALACES!) By The Worldwide People's Revolution!® Book 021B. Study it, O Fools!}

11-01 [_] ♦♦♦♦♦♦♦ Most People never stop to Think about WHY they have Pains in their Bodies; but, Pains are GOOD Warning Signs, which can Save you tens of thousands of Dollars, if you are Wise, and take Heed: beCause those Pains are Warning you that something is WRong, and must be Corrected. For Example, if someone is Twisting your Arm up behind your Back, and Causing you to have Pains in your Arm, or Shoulder, the Remedy is to STOP Twisting your Arm — NOT Consume a gallon of Pain-killing Pills, nor have the Doctor Knife cut off your Arm, nor Smoke Marijuana! Likewise, if you are Eating Foods that CAUSE you to have PAINS — such as Migraine Headaches from Eating Candies and Drinking Cokes — all you have to Do is STOP Eating Candies and

Drinking Cokes: beCause the REFINED SUGAR is the Chief Enemy, which does not Require the Diagnostic Surveys of Medical Doctors (Legalized Snakes) to Understand that. †§‡

11-02 [_] So, O Selected King, are you saying that if we have Headaches, it could be Caused by SUGAR? What about STRESS, Worries, FEARS, Unemployment, Homelessness, Extreme Poverty, and all of those other Capitalist Blessings, which you are so Fond of, O Rooster? †§‡§§

11-03 [_] Well, my Sarcastic Friend, that is what makes it so Tricky to Diagnose what Ails People: beCause a Headache could also be Caused by Red Garden Beets, Hot Peppers, Beers, Wines, and other Irritants within our Bowels. Therefore, if you have a Headache, the First Remedy, and the most Effective in most Cases, is to simply take an ENEMA, whereby Pure Water Flushes Out your Lower Bowels, along with those Irritants. Indeed, you could also have a Headache from being Constipated with Cheese, Grease, Butter, Bread, and Especially MEATS, Eggs, and even very Dry Dates, which are not very Laxative. Therefore, you must Study your own Body, in Order to Understand it: beCause the Doctor Knife seems to be Totally Unaware of the CAUSES for your Ailments, in spite of Operating on People who are Filled with STINKING FILTH, whereby his own Nostrils should Warn him of the DANGERS: beCause STINK is also a Warning Sign along the Highway of Life. Indeed, you might have Noticed that almost every Mammal in the World is Wise enough to Smell of its own Dung, and Especially if it is a Horse, Cat, or Dog, who are more Intelligent than some People, who Flush it down the Toilet Drain as quickly as Possible: beCause of the STINK. However, when Sick People go into Hospitals, their Wastes — both Piss and Dung — are often Microscopically Examined for "Dietary Sins," Special Bacterias, and Germs, whereby whatever Ails you can be Discovered! †‡

11-04 [_] So, O Dr. Sam, are you Recommending that we should Squat over our Dinner Plates, and Piss into our Drinking Glasses, so as to Examine our Wastes after every Bowel Movement?§

11-05 [_] NO! — I am just saying that we should be AWARE of the Conditions of our own Bowels, which should not be Filled with Sticky Gooey Turkey Dressings, nor similar Stuffings: beCause it is not Healthy. After all, if we are Seeking Good Health, it begins with having CLEAN Bowels, as Jesus was telling the Scribes and Pharisees, who had Ears; but, their Ears were Full of the Wax of Unbelief, whereby they could not Hear Spiritual Things, including Similes and Metaphors, which are somewhat Explained in the Public School of Ignorant FOOLS, in "High School," which just Touches on the Subject. †‡ {See www.Amazon.com for: "The Public School of IGNERUNT FQLZ!" (HOW we have been GRAATLEE DISEEVD by Capitalism!) By The Worldwide People's Revolution!® Book 024B, which is a Companion Book of: "In thu Beeginingz uv Thingz!" (Thu Kreeaashun Stooree frum thu Beegining!) By The Worldwide People's Revolution!® Book 025B. Otherwise, you will just have to Remain in the Darkness of Ignorance, along with the Doctor Pill Popper, Dr. Pus Shooter, Dr. Niif, Dr. Mental Disorder, Dr. Nerve Killer, and a hundred other Kinds of SPECIALISTS, and People who Know much more than GOD, who is "… that Stupid Old Man up in the Sky, who has no Idea what he is Talking about." †§‡§§}

11-06 [_] O Dr. Samuel Walker Edison, I say that you should be Arrested and brought to Court for Teaching Lies, and for Badmouthing our Public Schools, which are the Best Schools in all of the World, which Graduate High School Students, who cannot even "Reed" nor "Riit." § {See the KEE TQ PROONUNSEEAASHUN in the Appendix for: "LIGHTNING STRIKES Versus Lightning Bugs!" (HOW you can Become Moderately RICH, without Telling any Lies nor Selling any Trash!) By The Worldwide People's Revolution!® Book 074, which is a Companion Book of: "LIGHTNING **Versus the** Lightning Bug!" (HOW almost Everyone can become Moderately RICH, without Telling Any Lies nor Selling Any Capitalist Trash!) By The Worldwide People's Revolution!® Book 001B, which is a Companion Book of: "LIGHTNING STRIKES Versus Lightning Bugs and Impotent Fireflies!" (A Memorial Photo Album of some Real American Heroes!) By The Worldwide People's Revolution!® Book 072, which is a Companion Book of: "The BEST of CAPITALISM!" (Corrections for: "LIGHTNING STRIKES Versus Lightning Bugs and Impotent Fireflies!") Book 073, which is a Companion Book of: "How GAY is GOD?" (Oh, the Wonders of it all, when it ALL Hangs Out!) By The Worldwide People's Revolution!® Book 071, all of which are Designed by God to Drive us all CRAZY with Lightning Strikes, unless we Humble ourselves by Means of Fasting and Praying for the Forgiveness of Mistreating those Poor American Indians, and those Poor Black Africans, some of whom knew more about Good Health, than those Medical Snakes, who should Carefully Study: "What is The GREATEST SIN?" (And it is NOT Blasphemy Against the Holy Spirit!) By The Worldwide People's Revolution!® Book 091, plus: "HOW to Make Proper REPARATIONS!" (True Justice for Black and White People, and Everyone in Between them!) **By The**

Worldwide People's Revolution!® Book 122. Yes, that will Light your Fires, O Deceived Capitalist SLAVES, who have Surely Suffered Long Enough! [_] AMEN!}

11-07 [_] So, O Dr. Sam, if our Bowels were Clean, we would not have anything to Wipe Off, even as we Learned in Chapter 01, riit?

11-08 [_] ♦♦ You must be thinking of Verse 021-12-33 in **"The LUSCIOUS All-Mineral Organic Method of Gardening!"** Yes, that Good Book has much to say about Good Health, which everyone should Study, except for Greedy Medical Doctors, who do not Deserve to Discover WHY they are so Hungry for Money, and can never be Satisfied, no matter how much they might EAT. †§‡ (See *Micah 6:14,* and *Jeremiah 46:11.*) {WARNING: The Original Edition of that Good Book is not the same as the Updated Version, which is Available. Indeed, my MicroSOFT Computer Program was Updated in such a Way that it DELETED all of the Original Books! So, I am Unable to Update them without Writing NEW Books, which I have done for most of them; but, not all: beCause these Things Require TIME. Moreover, I Suffered with Carbon Monoxide Poisoning, when I was in the United States Army, whereby I Lost my Memory. Therefore, no one can Expect me to Remember what all was in the Original Books, since I could not even Remember my own First Name, when I got my Honorable Discharge, without any Medical Pay for my Disability, not to Mention being Sprayed with Agent Orange, which gave to me Cancers. Therefore, beCause of being a Victim of Capitalism, I was never Able to get a Job with Poor Uncle Jobe: beCause, I could not Legally even Drive a Car: beCause I had hardly any Memory; but, by the Grace of God, I Drove for 50 Years without a Personal Driver's License: beCause I had to: beCause my Poor Brother Vern was Struck by some Government Satellite with some Mysterious Radiation, which Destroyed his Mind, and made him a Mental Wreck, whereby he could not even Remember where the Toilet was, and therefore Pissed in his Dawter-in-law's Milk Jug, which he found in her Refrigerator, which was the End of that Unholy Relationship, which put me in Charge of the Swanky Nursing Home for the next 30-plus Years, without a "Job" to Support us: beCause I only got to Work for just ONE Day for Wages during 50-plus Years; and that is the Truth of it! Nevertheless, just to Prove that God is Able and Willing to Care for his Servants, he Provided everything that I Needed for Prospering, by Creating Faithful Friends for me, who Supported me. Otherwise, I would have been another one of those Homeless People on the Streets of Lost Angels, Californicate, San Fransissies, Seattle, Houston, Dall-ass, Tex-ass, Sin-sinatee, Ohio, or in some other Hell Hole in "The Divided States of United Lies!" (The so-called "United States of North America" in Disguise!) **By The Worldwide People's Revolution!®** Book 058 — Thanks to that Irreverent LOUDMOUTH Sloth-gut Windbag Hole-in-his-Head, who never Preached so much as one Good Sermon about GOOD Government, and HOW to Obtain it: beCause, that Unholy Mutilated Bible was Missing: **"The Sixth Book of Moses called GOOD GOVERNMENT!"** (The Primary Missing Book in the Holy Bible!) **By The Worldwide People's Revolution!®** Book 126, which God has now Restored, which is Deliberately Designed to Confound those so-called "Wise Men" in Washington, District of Chief Criminals, who will Naturally be Mocking it; but, the Humble Honest Followers of the Lamb of God will be Praising it for its Goodness: beCause it is perhaps the "Goodest Book" ever Written! But, you do not have to Accept my Words for it, when you can Study it for yourself, O Humble Man of Greater Faith, who will also find it Difficult to Swallow, until you Reed it for the Third Time, and DO what it says to DO! Yes, that is when it will come ALIVE, O Mockingbirds, whereby you will be Singing a New Song of Great JOY! †§‡}

11-09 [_] So, O Dr. Sam, I see that you like to Tease those Medical Doctors, huh?

11-10 [_] ♦♦♦ Well, my Friend, I do Respect them for their Skills in being Able to Repair someone who has been Mangled in a Car Wreck, for Example, which is mostly the Work of the Doctor Knife, Doctor Procaine, Doctor Anesthesia, and Doctor Morphine, who have to Work Together on it. However, no such Cars are Needed for True Prosperity, and very few People would ever get that Mutilated, except in Wars, which are also as Needless as Teats on a Boar Hog, even though those Teats are probably more Needed than Wars, just to be Able to Refer to them as Metaphors. One of the Greatest Advantages for Building those **"GLORIOUS Swanky Hotels Castles and Fortresses!"** (Beautiful Planned City States for WISE Intelligent Well-Educated People with Common Sense and Good Understanding!) **By The Worldwide People's Revolution!®** Book 019B, is the Fact that they make Wars Obsolete: beCause it is Impossible to Conquer a Swanky Fortress from without the Borders: beCause of the DESIGNS, which God Revealed to our Selected King, about 40 Years Ago, TODAY! Yes, at that Time, he did not Know that there were more than 5,000 Good Reasons and Great Advantages for Building Beautiful Planned City STATES! But, now we have Discovered no less than 7 Billion Good Reasons, one of which is YOURSELF! †§‡

11-11 [_] So, O Dr. Sam, is it Fair to say that if we Eat nothing but Sweet Juicy Ripe Fruits, that our Dung will not Stink after a Year or 2 on such a Good Diet?

11-12 [_] Well, if you do enough Fasting and Eating nothing but Sweet Ripe Juicy Fruits between Fasts, neither your Bowels nor your Wastes will Stink afterwards. In Fact, you could "Dump" it on your Dinner Plate, and ask someone to Close their Eyes, while you hold the Plate behind your Back, and then ask them to keep their Eyes Closed, and Smell of it, so as to Identify what it might be: beCause not one Person on the Earth could Identify it as Normal Human Dung: beCause it would Smell like Fermented Fruits, only. (For God's Sake, do not Try it with your Mother-in-law, lest you should be hit on the Head with her Frying Pan, or even be Stabbed in the Back with her Butcher Niif: beCause she is also another Victim of Capitalism, who might be Super Sensitive!) †§‡

11-13 [_] Are you Kidding?

11-14 [_] No, I am Dead Serious! (No pun intended.) Just Try that Scientific Experiment, and you will Know the Truth of it; and that Truth will make you Free from the Lies that are Tawt in the Public School of Ignorant Fools. †‡

11-15 [_] My Mother-in-law would never Forgive me, if I used one of her Dinner Plates for that Scientific Experiment, much less, allow me to come into her House again, in spite of the Fact that her own Bathroom Sticks to the Highest Heaven, as they say, just after she has had a Bowel Movement, whereby she Sprays some Abominable "Deodorant," which Chemicals Smell Worse than a Dead Dog along the Highway during the Summertime, after being Dead for 3 or 4 Days: because those Chemicals Cause Brain Damage, which is also True of those Extremely Stinking "Cakes" that they put in Toilets and Urinals in "Rest Rooms" and in Dangerous Bathrooms! †§‡

11-16 [_] So, are you saying that your Mother-in-law has been reading her *Bible* for 40 Years, and has not yet Discovered that Verse that Clearly states that "NO UNCLEAN THING SHALL ENTER INTO THE HOLY KINGDOM OF ALL THAT IS GOOD"? ‡

11-17 [_] And just WHERE in the *Bible* is that Verse Located?

11-18 [_] Well, you can find it many Times from *Genesis* to *Revelation;* but, not in those Exact same Words: beCause those Exact Words are only found in the New MAGNIFIED Version (NMV), which I will Quote to you in Context in Chapter 12, which is one of the most Powerful Chapters in all of the *Bible.* (See *Leviticus 10:10; Chapter 11, 12:2, 5; Second Corinthians 6:17; 7:1; Ephesians 5:5; and Revelation 22:15.*)

11-19 [_] So, his Mother-in-law has been reading the *Bible* with a lowercase r, instead of a Capital R, riit?

11-20 [_] Well, that is Correct at the Core of it, and even on the Peeling of it; but, if your Mind has been Blinded by Traditional Religious LIES, whereby you still Deny that Stink is STINK, and Filth is FILTH, you do have a Major Problem in General, O Lieutenant Colonel Hiccups. †§‡§§

11-21 [_] So, O Dr. Sam, is it Fair to say that NOTHING in the Kingdom of God will be Stinking? Do Horses and Camels not Stink?

11-22 [_] Well, those Horses and Camels might have a certain Odor; but, not a Stink, like the Bad Breath of a Stinking Dog, nor like the Smell of Hog Dung, whereby you can smell Swines a Mile Away, as Nigger Jim might say, after Cleaning Out the Hog Pens. Indeed, some Things are a little Smelly, while other Things STINK — such as Snakes and Skunks and many other "Unclean" Creatures, none of which will Enter into the Government of the Gods, who are HOLY. ‡ {See: **"HOW to Become a HOLY Man!" (40 Good Reasons WHY People Should FAST and PRAY!) By The Worldwide People's Revolution!® Book 045.}**

11-23 [_] So, O Dr. Sam, can that be Proven in a Courtroom? Will the *Holy Bible* be put on Trial for its Professed "Truths," and Outlandish LIES?

11-24 [_] Yes, that can be Proven in a Courtroom. Moreover, all Books should be put on Trial for their Goodness, including this one, and the Evil Books should be Disposed of by FIRE: beCause God HATES them, and so should we; but, only God has a Right to Judge them, if he Inspired them. †§‡ (Please Check the Box, if you Agree.)

11-25 [_] So, O Doctor Samuel Walker Edison, WHO would be the Judge of the Goodness of any Book, including this one, since God has gone to Sleep?

11-26 [_] Well, my Friend, if it can be Proven that there are any Lies in the *Holy Bible,* for Example, those Lies can be Deleted or Corrected, so as to make it a Good Book. Yes, if there are any Provable Lies within this Inspired Book, those Lies should be Corrected. Therefore, if you Think that you have Discovered any such Lies, please make a Note of it in the Margins, and Remind us of it, so as to Correct them: beCause we would not Want to Burn the Truths with the Lies, when they only need to be Removed or Cleaned Out, and Separated from Godly Sarcasms. †§‡§§

11-27 [_] So, O Doctor Sam, we would not Destroy the entire Book, just beCause of Discovering one little Lie, would we?

11-28 [_] That is Correct — we would Certainly NOT Do any such Evil Things. However, there are some books that do not contain any Truths worth Remembering, which Books should be GRADED as follows, for their Goodness, or Evilness:

A-[_] Extremely Good, (♦) Diamond Rating.

B-[_] Exceptionally Good, (♥) Heart Rating.

C-[_] Good, (★) Star Rating.

D-[_] Fair, (■) Square Rating.

E-[_] Poor, (▲) Triangular Rating.

F-[_] Bad, (● / ◗) Solid Dot or Half-moon Rating.

G-[_] Very Bad, (♣) Club Rating, or:

H-[_] Extremely Bad (♠) with a Spade Rating!

11-29 [_] So, O Dr. Sam, is it Fair to say that everyone and everything in the Whole World can be Graded by those 8 Grades? Is the Confusing Tale of the Colorful Peacock from Angel Rij, at King's Mountain, Kentucky 40442 U.S.A., a BAD Thing, which should be given an Extremely Bad Rating with a Black Spade, just for Upsetting the Great False Economy; or, does it Rate with the Best of Literature ever Written? Indeed, if you become the Elected King of **"The New RIGHTEOUS One-World Government!" (HOW to Establish a Righteous One-World Government without Going to WAR!) By The Worldwide People's Revolution!®** Book 056, and some Ignorant Fool gives your Books a Spade Rating, you are likely to have his or her Head Removed with **"The Swanky Sword of Divine Truths!" (The Most-Powerful**

Weapon in the Whole Universe!) By The Worldwide People's Revolution!® Book 067, which could Prove to be a Real Bloodbath in Saint Peter's Basilica, in Rome, where you and your Fellow Agitators will Conduct: "The GREAT Worldwide TELEVISED Court HEARING!" (That Great Meeting of the Most-Intelligent and Well-Educated Minds!) By The Worldwide People's Revolution!® Book 041B.

11-30 |_| Yes, every Person, Animal, Tree, Book, Sentence, Building, Bridge, Material, Tool, Toy, Game, Sport, Religion, and Political Belief can be Graded as such. But, as for any Bloodbath in Rome, it is very Unlikely: beCause 99.999,999,999% of the People in this World of Wonders will Agree with our Selected King, who will be the Person who has the Best "Guaranteed Solutions!" (HOW to Solve our Local and Global Problems in the Most-Rational Manner Possible!) By The Worldwide People's Revolution!® Book 080. Indeed, "All of the Arguments are in Favor of our Selected King, who has Zero Challengers!" (Before you Attend another Election Deception, you should Carefully Study this Inspired Book with an Honest Open Mind!) By The Worldwide People's Revolution!® Book 085. Therefore, unless you have some Really STRONG Arguments against his Master Plan, you should be Wise, and "VOTE for The GOAT!" (The New Political Party that has Guaranteed Solutions for our Massive Problems!) By The Worldwide People's Revolution!® Book 109: beCause, this is "The END of CONFUSION!" (The Great CELEBRATION of the Magnificent Wedding of the Most-Humble, Honest Nations, and the Grand Year of JUBILEE!) By The Worldwide People's Revolution!® Book 050.

— Chapter 12 —

The New MAGNIFIED Version of John 3 in Plain English ♦

12-01 [_] Now, there was a certain Man of the Sect of the Pharisees, named Nicodemus, a Ruler among the Jews, who came to the Anointed Savior during the Night, in Secret, and said to him: "Master, we Know that you are a Good Teacher, who has Come from God: because no Man can Do all of the Miracles that you Do, except that God is with him. Therefore, I am Wondering how that I can get the Gifts that you have?"

12-02 [_] Jesus Answered him, "Truly, truly, I say to you: **Except a Man should be Born Again, he cannot even Visualize nor Understand the Holy Kingdom of the Supreme Ruler."**

12-03 [_] Therefore, Nicodemus said to him, "How can a Man be Born when he is Old? — can he Enter into his Mother's Womb for the Second Time, and be Born Again? Do you Accept the Doctrine of those People who Live in the East, in India, who say that we have all Lived before: because it is Impossible for a Person to Learn all of his Lessons during only one Lifetime; and therefore, it Requires many Lives, in Order to Learn such Lessons?"

12-04 [_] Jesus Answered, "Truly, Truly, I say to you: Except a Man should be Born of Water from the Womb, and also Born of the Spirit from the Womb of God, he cannot Enter into the Holy Kingdom of the Most-High Ruler: because each Man must be Tested in the Furnace of Afflictions, in Order for the Creator to Discover which ones are Worthy to Enter into his Righteous Kingdom. Indeed, they who are Born of the Flesh are Flesh and Blood, who are Born by Water from the Womb; and they who are Born of the Spirit are Spiritual: because the Heavenly Father Adopts them into his Holy Family, which is a Spiritual Family, which has One Mind, One Understanding, One Opinion, One Agreement, One Great Hope, One Faith, One Baptism by Fire, One Great Purpose, and One Love — who all Love each other as a Truly United Family of Holy Ones. Therefore, do not Marvel that I said to you, that you must be Born Again: because all People must be Born Again of Water and Spirit, before they can Enter into the Holy Kingdom of the Most-High God, unless they are Perfected during this Lifetime, in which

Case they will not have to Live here Again, until the Resurrection at the End of the Ages: because they have Passed their Tests of Nolij, Faith, Hope, Trust, Patience, Love, and Obedience. Indeed, the Wind Blows wherever it Desires, and you can Hear the Sound that it Makes; but, you cannot tell where it Comes from, nor where it Goes to. Likewise, so is every Person who is Born of the Spirit, which Comes like the Wind, which Transforms the Mind of Man, and Makes him like a New Creature: because Old Things have Passed Away; and behold, all Things are NEW: because he who Humbles himself by Means of Fasting and Praying, and Confesses all of his Sins, and Cleanses himself from all Filthiness of his Mind and Body, is Purged from all Uncleanness from Head to Toe, and is therefore Physiologically and Spiritually Born Again: because he is Filled with the Holy Spirit, who can only Live within Clean Temples, and not just Visit them on Special Occasions; but, **no Unclean Thing can Enter Into the Holy Kingdom of All that is GOOD**. Nevertheless, that Holy Spirit can Visit any Temple, even if it is Unclean: because she Draws People to our Heavenly Father. Therefore, if People only Sincerely Confess their Sins, and Repent to that Degree, they are Blest with a Portion of his Holy Spirit: because he must let them Know that he Loves them, just for Encouragement. Therefore, his Holy Spirit Enters Into them for a certain Length of Time, just in Order to let them Know that they are Headed in the Right Direction, even if they are Hindus or Buddhists. Nevertheless, they cannot have the Fullness of his Holy Spirit, until they are Holy, which Means that they must be Pure in Mind and Body, even as I am Pure: because I am your Good Example, who can also Do Miracles in Order to Prove it."

12-05 [_] And Nicodemus said to him, "How can those Things be? How can the Holy Spirit Judge who is Worthy of her Spirit, and who is not Worthy?? Are not all Children Born Holy? Must they also Repent by Means of Fasting and Praying, as you say?"

12-06 [_] And Jesus Answered him, "Blest are the Innocent Holy Children, like Baby Moses, who was a Proper Child: because, of such are the Kingdom of the Gods. Are you a Master of Israel, and do not Know those Basic Truths? Did John the Baptist not Teach to you all of those Good Lessons? Truly, Truly, I say to you: We Speak of that which we Do Know, and we Testify of that which we have Seen; and yet you Scribes and Pharisees do not Accept our Witness to those Great Truths: because you have not Fasted Sufficiently, nor Earnestly Prayed for Forgiveness for ALL of your Sins, including your Dietary Sins, which Prevent you from Understanding my Words. However, if I have told you about Earthly Things, and you do not Believe, how shall you Believe, if

I tell you about Heavenly Things? And Remember this, **NO Man has Ascended up to Heaven**, to the Throne of the Most-High Ruler, except he who Came Down from Heaven, even the Son of a Holy Man, who is a Chosen Son of the Most-High Ruler, who is in Heaven, who Chose that Man to Bear the Holy Seed from which I was Conceived within the Womb of a Holy Wombman, by the Power of the Holy Spirit, which Came on my Parents as they Slept, and Transferred that Holy Seed from the Loins of my Father Yoseph, into the Womb of my Mother Maryam, before they had Sexual Intercourse: because it was Appointed unto them to be Blest with a Holy Child, who would become the Savior of the People of the World, even to as many as will Accept him and Obey his Inspired Words of Provable Truths.

12-07 [_] "Indeed, as Moses Lifted Up the Brass Serpents in the Wilderness, so that all Men who had been Bitten by Poisonous Serpents might Look upon them, and be Saved Alive, even so the Son of a Holy Man must also be Lifted Up, so that everyone can be Saved from their Sins, who Look upon him, whose Minds have been Poisoned by that Old Serpent, the Devil, who has Successfully Deceived almost all Men by Subtle Means, who Wears a Multi-colored Coat of Deceptions, whose Head is filled with Poisonous Lies, who Strikes at the Colorful Peacock with the Poisonous Fangs of Hate and Revenge, whose Chief Servants are Medical Doctors, who Drug the Ignorant Uneducated People, whereby they are Greatly Deceived. Nevertheless, whosoever Believes in the Son of a certain Man, and Obeys his Lovable Words of Divine Truths, will not Perish; but, will have Everlasting Good Health: beCause I am Come so that you might have Good Health, and have it more Abundantly: because the Supreme Ruler Loved the People of the World so much, that he Gave his only Chosen Son, who was Begotten by the Power of the Holy Spirit, so that whosoever Truly and Sincerely Believes in him should not Perish, even as they did not Perish when Moses was here; but, have Everlasting Good Health, which is also Everlasting Life: because the Supreme Ruler did not Send his Son into the World, in Order to Condemn the People of the World; but, so that the People of the World might be Saved through Faith in him, by his Grace and Mercy, by Humble Obedience to his Words of Truths: beCause, without Grace and Mercy, there was no Binding Promise that he should Come, nor even Teach anyone anything about Life, Love, Happiness, nor any Good Thing: beCause all of those Good Things Come beCause of Grace and Mercy: beCause our Heavenly Father is Full of Grace and Mercy: beCause of his Great Love for his Potential Children, who may be Adopted into his Holy Family, which is Revealed by his Only Begotten Son.

12-08 [_] "Therefore, he who Believes on him who was Sent to Save them, is not Condemned; but, he who does not Believe in him, is Condemned already: beCause he has not Believed in the Name of the Only Son who was Begotten by the Power of the Holy Spirit, who is the Female Part of the Godhead, you might say. Moreover, this is the Condemnation, that Light and Truth have Come into the World; but, Unclean Men have Loved the Darkness of Ignorance, rather than the Light of Truths: beCause their Thoughts and Deeds are Evil. Indeed, every Person who Does Evil, HATES the Light of Truths; and will not Come to the Light, lest his Evil Deeds should be Discovered, and his Sins are Exposed; but, he who Does Good, Comes to the Light of Truths, so that his Good Deeds might be made Known, that they are Worked According to the Will of the Supreme Ruler, who would have all People to Do Good Works, rather than to Do Evil Works: beCause there is no Profit nor Gain by Doing Evil Works: beCause Evil Deeds Breed more and more Evil Deeds, until at Last all of the People are Suffering under the Tyrannical Dominion of an Evil Empire, which makes Tax Slaves of those Unwise People, who could simply Obey the Laws of the Master Farmer, and be FREE from all such Slavery; but, instead, they Willfully Choose to Do Evil, and therefore they get their Just Rewards. And now, to Answer your Question — 'Are not all Children Born Holy?' — you can See that they are NOT: beCause, if they were, they would be like me, or like Moses and Elijah; but, instead, some of them are like little Demons: because they are Born from Unholy Parents. Indeed, each Tree Produces Fruit like itself."

12-09 [_] Then Nicodemus said to Jesus, "Are you saying that a Good Government would not have any Taxes? If so, WHO would Pay for the Services of Government Officials and their Armies?"

12-10 [_] And Jesus Answered him, "Truly, Truly, I say to you, that a Righteous GovernMint would simply Mint the Necessary Silver and Gold Coins, in Order to Use that New Money Wisely, in Order to Hire whomever is Willing and Able to Learn and Work, in Order to Help Build their own Secure Stone Dome Homes with Polished Marble Walls, Home-craft Workshops with Polished Granite Floors, Fruit Tree Houses with Removable Glass- and Steel-covered Roofs, Rock Walls for Retaining the Topsoil around their All-Mineral Organic Gardens, Tunnels for Convenience and Security, Cisterns for Water Storage, Stone Walls for Terraced Gardens, Root Cellars, Ice Houses with Walk-in Coolers surrounding them, Honeybee Houses, Bat Houses, and whatever they Need, in Order to Live and Work and Prosper, at Home; and that Stonework would Represent that New Money, which would have to be

Earned by Honest Labor, with all Men being Paid EQUAL WAGES for EQUAL SERVICES, According to a List of Fair Wages, which would make that Money just as Valuable as the Effort that it would Require to Earn it; and therefore, all Working Soldiers within that Righteous Kingdom could Obtain their own Beautiful Tax-free Loan-free Usury-free Stone Dome Home Complexes, at Cost, if they were Willing and Able to Learn and Work, which includes almost all People, who could Voluntarily Join many Great Armies of Working Soldiers, until all such Houses are Built within Beautiful Planned City States. Moreover, when all of the People Learn to Love and Obey ALL of my Commandments, there will be NO Stealing, NO Murdering, NO Raping, NO Robbing, and no Need for Collecting any Taxes: because all of those Wise People will LOVE their Leaders, and will therefore Gladly Support them by Means of Freewill Offerings and Donations, or Tithes, even as Moses was Supported: because there are very few Officials Needed within such a Righteous Kingdom, which does not Need to Maintain an Army of Defenders: beCause WHO can Overcome them, if they Build Proper Cities, which have all of the Gardens, Vineyards, Orchards, Houses, Homecraft Workshops and Sales Shops within the Borders of their STRONG Fortified Planned City States? Yes, WHO can Attack them and Overcome them, once they are Thoroughly Dug in, with Tunnels, Moats, Cisterns, and whatever Stone Walls and Iron Gates that they Need, in Order to Defend themselves? Truly, Truly, I say to you, only a General Fool would even Contemplate such an Attack: because it would be Futile and Self-defeating: because no such Fortified City can be Overcome by any Small Means, and is certainly not Worth the Great Expense of Trying to Overcome it: because each House and Workshop would be Equally as Strong as a Fortress, itself. Therefore, the Wise People will Foresee the Evils that are Coming, and thus, get themselves Prepared for the Worst Conditions: because it is Possible for the Worst to Happen to them, just in Order to Test their Knowledge, Faith, Hope, Trust, Patience, Love and Obedience: because the Devil Rules Over the Kingdoms of this World, and he Inspires some of them to go to War; but, WHO can make War Against the Holy City of the Great King, which is Guarded by the Invisible Holy Angels?"

12-11 [_] And Nicodemus said to him, "Are you that Great King who is to Come during these Last Days, in Order to Establish your Good GovernMint Over all Nations under Heaven; or, should we Look for someone else, and have Faith in some other Person who might Speak more Plainly than yourself?"

12-12 [_] And Jesus Answered him, "Truly, Truly, I say to you, that I was Born to be a Great King, who shall Rule Over all Peoples of all Nations of this World with a Rod of Iron; but, not until I have Established my Kingdom within the Hearts and Minds of all Men who might Believe in me, who must Learn to Rule Over themselves, and Conquer the Beastly Nature within themselves: because that is the Dreaded Enemy, which everyone should Fear the Most: because, if that Beast is not Overcome, the Devil will have Rulership Over you. Therefore, let every Man Strive to Overcome all of his Sins, and to STOP Sinning: beCause all such Sins Separate you from the Supreme Ruler, who will Establish his Holy Kingdom during these Last Days: beCause there is a Great Day of Peaceful Rest Coming, even that Great Sabbath Day, which is the Seventh Day; but, be not Ignorant of this one Important Thing — that One Day to the Supreme Ruler is a Thousand Years, and a Thousand Years is One Day. Therefore, when Six Thousand Years have Passed Away since the Beginning, when Adam was Formed from the Dust of the Ground, after which Adam and Eve were Cast Out of the Paradise of Peace and Happiness, there will be a Great Day of Peaceful Rest, at which Time I will Rule the World. Yes, there will be a Holy One-World Government, which will not Need Money: because everyone will have True Love for everyone else; and therefore, all Peoples will have all Material Things in Common. That is, they will Share their Time, Materials, Energy, and Possessions with each other, until all are Moderately Rich in all Ways. Nevertheless, Before that Day of Rest, there will be a New Righteous One-World Government, which will Do what I said before, and Mint and/or Print the Necessary New Money, in Order to Use that Money Wisely, in Order to Hire **Seven Great Armies of Working Soldiers**, in Order to Build Various Kinds of Stone Dome Homes and other Stone Structures for themselves, so that they might also become Moderately Rich: because there will Come a Time when Nolij will be Greatly Increased, and this Good News will be Published to all Peoples in all Nations: because it is Necessary, in Order to Save those Wise People who will Believe and Obey my Inspired Words of Provable Truths."

12-13 [_] And Nicodemus said to him, "You Speak with Riddles, O Master House Builder, which no one can Understand. Indeed, are you saying that you will Live for another 3,000 Years!?"

12-14 [_] And Jesus said to him, "Are you a Master in Israel, and do not Know the Scriptures? Truly, Truly, I say to you, the Master House Builder will be Judged and Condemned by the Scribes and Pharisees of this Generation, who will Envy him for his Goodness, who will Arrange for his Death; but, behold, after Three Nights and Three Days, he will

Arise from the Dead, even as it is Written in the Psalms of King David, who told about my Passing Through the Valley of the Shadow of Death."

12-15 [_] And Nicodemus said to him, "You must be Insane, to Think that King David was Referring to you, rather than to himself, only: because there is no Mention of any Great King in that Psalm."

12-16 [_] To which Jesus Responded, "If King David were here, Today, he would tell you that he Foresaw my Time, and how that I would be Persecuted and Tortured by my Enemies, who Naturally Assume that I am Insane; but, how many Insane People can Do Miracles, such as you have Heard about, from Eye Witnesses, who have not Denied that I am in Deed that Great King; but, you do not Wholeheartedly Believe in me: because you are Blinded by your Pride and Ignorance. Yes, you are a Better Person than those other Scribes and Pharisees: because you at least Seek the Truth; but, **because of your Ignorance concerning the Scriptures, you will also Stumble Over my Inspired Words of Provable Truths.** Nevertheless, when the Son of a Man shall Rise Up from the Dead, then you will Believe and Obey. Yes, you will also become one of my Humble Disciples: beCause I Knew you Before you were Born into this World, even Before you were Conceived within the Womb of your Mother: beCause I am the Master Farmer of this World, and I Made you, myself, by the Power of my Heavenly Father, some of whose Truths you Reject: beCause you Reject the Words of his Only Chosen Son in this World, who was Begotten by the Power of his Holy Spirit. Therefore, do yourself a Great Favor, and STUDY all of those Scriptures as if they were TRUE: beCause they are True, and they do Speak of me: beCause I have Come in Order to Fulfill the Scriptures, and to make all Things PLAIN and EASY to Understand." And Nicodemus Turned himself Away and Disappeared into the Darkness of Ignorance, you might say: because we are surrounded by Ignorance on all Sides.

12-17 [_] After those Events, Jesus and his Disciples came into the Land of Judea, where he Stayed with his Disciples while they all Fasted and Prayed, until their Minds and Bodies were somewhat Purified, even as his was Pure; but, not all: because some Disciples Needed to Do much more Fasting; and he also Baptized them with Water, after they were Purged from their Filthiness by Feasting on Fresh Sweet Fruits and Grape Juice. Moreover, John the Baptist was also Baptizing at that Time in Enon, which is near to Salim: beCause there was much Water there, which was Used in Order to Immerse the People in the Water, after they did their Repenting, According to the Law of Repentance, which Requires that we Fast and Pray until our Minds and Bodies are Purified:

because that is the Strait and Narrow Way that Leads to Everlasting Good Health, which few People ever Discover: because they Refuse to Believe the Inspired Words of Provable Truths, which Jesus has Taught to us, saying: *"Except an Unclean Man should Humble himself by Means of Fasting and Praying, until he becomes like an Innocent Child with a Clean Mind and a Purified Body, he shall in no Way Enter Into the Holy Kingdom of All that is Good."* Therefore, John came Preaching that Same Message, in Order to Prepare the Way for the Master Farmer, who Arrived shortly after John, Preaching the very Same Message of Repentance. However, John Baptized *anyone* unto Repentance, even before they became Holy in Mind and Body: because it was Symbolical of that Purification, which was a Great Threat to the Evil Empire: because it Caused People to Understand what is Needful in this World, which is not all of those Vain Things of the World, which you can see for Sale in Junk Stores; but, it is Gardens and Fruit Trees: beCause the Life of Mankind is Found in the Sweet Juicy Fruits, which any Person can Discover, if he or she simply Fasts and Prays, until his or her Tongue is Clean, or until his or her Tastebuds are Working Correctly. Therefore, John Understood it: because he did much Fasting and Praying, along with his True Disciples. Furthermore, he was not yet Cast into Prison at this Time: beCause his Appointed Hour had not yet Come, According to the Master Plan of the Master Farmer, who has a Set Time for all Divine Things, which will all be Fulfilled in Due Season.

12-18 [ ] Then there Arose a certain Question between some of John's Disciples and the Jews about the Purifying of the Mind and Body. And they came to John, and said to him, "Master, behold, he who was with you beyond the River Jordan, to whom you Bear Witness, has Baptized his own Disciples, who are also Baptizing all of the People who come to them. Moreover, they are Teaching all of the People that they must Repent like the Men and Wombmen of Nineveh did, who Fasted for 40 Nights and 40 Days, Continuously, with Various Daily Washings, and Purifying their Bowels with Water, by taking Daily Enemas, after they Fasted until it was too Uncomfortable to Tolerate it, According to the Teachings of that Holy Man who has Come Among us, who says that he has also taken such a Long Fast, which Gives to him the Power and Authority that he has: beCause he Obeyed the Holy Spirit, and was therefore Blest with Gifts. Therefore, should we Believe on him, or in you?"

12-19 [ ] And John Answered, "A Man can Receive nothing from the Creator, except it is Given to him from the Throne of the Most-High Ruler. Indeed, you yourselves Bear Witness for me, that I said, *'I am not the Anointed One'*; but, that *'I am Sent Before him, in Order to Prepare the Way in Front of him,'* to which you must Agree: beCause I have hundreds of Self-disciplined Ones, in Order to Prove it, who also Accept the Anointed One: beCause we Teach the Same Great Truths, and Baptize for the very Same Purpose. However, he who has Control of the Heart of the Bride is the Bridegroom, who is the Anointed One, whose Bride is the Congregation of Believers; but, the Friend of the Bridegroom, who Stands Beside him and Listens to him, Rejoices with Gladness beCause of the Voice of the Bridegroom: beCause he Loves him, who also Loves him: beCause he is his Best Friend, or Beloved Spiritual Brother. Therefore, my Joy is Fulfilled in him, who is my Best Friend. Nevertheless, he must Increase with Power and Authority: beCause he is the Great King; but, I must Decrease, and at Last be Martyred for my Beliefs. Therefore, he who Comes from Above, from the Father of Lights, who Lives in the Highest Heaven on the Greatest Earth, is Above all People; but, he who Comes from this Earth, is Earthly, and Speaks of the Earth, and of the Things of this World: beCause he Understands them; but, he who Comes from Heaven is Above all Peoples, and is Worthy of our Praise and Attention. Therefore, whatever he has Seen and Heard, he Testifies to us: beCause he Loves us; and yet no Unclean Man, who is Destined for Destruction, Receives or Accepts his Testimony; and there are many of them, who will Multiply during the Last Days, just before the Second Coming of the Anointed Savior as the KING of Kings and SUPREME RULER of all Rulers. However, he who has Accepted his Testimony, and Obeyed his Loving Voice, has Set to his Seal that the Supreme Ruler of this Solar System is True, and has Kept his Promise: beCause he whom the Supreme Ruler has Sent, Speaks the Inspired Words of the Most-High God: beCause the Most-High Ruler does not Give the Holy Spirit by Measure to him; but, he Fills him with his Spirit: beCause the Heavenly Father Loves the Perfectly Obedient Son, and has Given all Things into his Control, in Order to Do as he Wills it. Therefore, he who Believes on that Holy Son, and Obeys his Father's Holy Spirit, has Everlasting Good Health, and will at Last be Given a Place within his Holy Kingdom; but, he who does not Believe his Divine Words of Inspired Truths, shall not even Visualize what it Means to have Good Health; but, he or she will be Blinded to the Truth, and will also Suffer for his or her Great Unbelief: beCause the Wrath of the Supreme Ruler Abides on him, who will be Sick and Diseased beCause of his Disobedience, even though he will be Blest for whatever Good Things that he has Spoken and Done. Therefore, if we Desire that Happiness, which Comes from Obeying the Great Master Farmer, we must Humble ourselves by Means of Fasting and Praying, even as Jesus Humbled himself in the Wilderness for 40 Days and 40

Nights, who did not Eat Food during that Time: beCause it was Necessary for him to Set a Good Example for us to Follow; and therefore, if it were Necessary for him who was Born from Holy Parents, to Fast and Pray for 40 Long Days and 40 Long Nights, then how much more Necessary is it for those Unclean People, who were not Born from Holy Parents? Truly, Truly, I say to you, Except you are Physiologically and Spiritually Born Again, even as Jesus Teaches, you cannot be Saved for Positions within his Holy Kingdom: because those Positions are Reserved for those Wise People who are Found Worthy, who are not Filthy Sinners like those Lying Edomites, who Commit Adultery in Secret, who Lust after the Vain Things of this World, and Deprive themselves of the Love of our Heavenly Father, who Fills us Honest White Jews with the Spirit of Love and JOY when we Learn and Obey ALL of his Commandments."

12-20 [_] So, are those the Pure Words of the Living God, O Dr. Sam?

12-21 [_] Well, you may Judge the Words for yourself. Are they in Agreement with the *Scriptures,* or not??

12-22 [_] Well, that could only be Proven in a Courtroom, where all of the Evidence is Presented by Honest Lawyers. However, suppose it is Proven, will we all have to Accept it as *Scriptures,* or else be Crucified for our Unbelief, or perhaps be Stoned to Death? †‡

12-23 [_] No, no one would have to Accept it as the Truth; but, everyone would be Wise to do so: beCause it could Prove to be rather Em-bare-assing during the Day of Judgment, when God Opens all of the Inspired Books, including this one, and asks you, WHY you did not Accept it?

12-24 [_] I See what you Mean. Indeed, it would not be very Wise of us to Reject any Truth without a Just Cause; and no one could Name any Just Causes for Rejecting those *Scriptures.* So, you have Trapped us, O Elected King, and there is no Way of Escape from the Truths that we have Learned. Indeed, once the Seeds of Truths have been Sown in the Gardens of our Lives, we can never get them Out of it, Thank God, or else we would Die a Great Spiritual Death, which is the Second Death. Therefore, God have Mercy on us, and Help us to Overcome all of our Sins, and Stop Sinning, lest we should be Cast Down into a Lower Order of Worlds with those Witchdoctors, Wicked Lawyers, Corrupt Politicians, Unjust Judges, Tax Masters, False Preachers, Misguided Teachers, Liars and Deceivers, who are Unworthy of any Positions in the Holy Kingdom of All that is GOOD. †‡

— Chapter 13 —

The Conclusion

13-01 [_] Surely there is a Mountain of Boring Evidence that could be Presented within this Boring Book, which would Condemn most Medical Doctors to Hell and Gone, no? †‡

13-02 [_] Well, we would not Want to make the Graveyard Mistake of Condemning ALL Medical Doctors, as if they were all alike, when there are no doubt some Good Honest Doctors, who will Naturally Assist People to do their Fasting, and to do it Properly, according to the RULES. Indeed, there is now more Need for GOOD Honest Doctors, than ever.

13-03 [_] So, did God or Satan Ordain Medical Doctors?

13-04 [_] Well, what do you Think, after Reading this Inspired Book? Would God Need any Kind of Drugs?

13-05 [_] If God did not Need any Kind of Drugs, WHY did he Create them in this World of Wonders?

13-06 [_] Well, I Maintain that Satan's Servants Planted them here, if they are Natural Drugs — such as Cocaine, Opium, Marijuana and Tobacco. Moreover, if they are Synthetic Drugs, I say that Satan Inspired People to Invent them, even as he Inspired the Automobiles and Televisions, which are only Good if they are used for Good Purposes. Otherwise, they should be done away with. †‡

13-07 [_] So, is Medical Marijuana a Good and Useful Drug?

13-08 [_] Well, it can likely be Proven in a Courtroom, along with everything else. Therefore, why do we, the People, not Try that Plan, and put the most Riichus Men in Charge of it? I Volunteer to be an Unbiased Judge. {See www.Amazon.com for: "The GREAT Worldwide TELEVISED Court HEARING!," which is the one and only Reasonable Solution for Solving our Massive Problems, by Learning the Whole Truth about all Important Subjects.}

13-09 [_] O Dr. Sam, I will Vote for you, if your Name ever gets on the Ballot.

13-10 [_] Well, just Do what Moses Tawt in: "The Sixth Book of Moses called GOOD GOVERNMENT!" (The Primary Missing Book in the Holy Bible!) By The Worldwide People's Revolution!® Book 126, who Revealed how to get around those Election Deceptions. ‡

{All Young People could be in Equally as Good Health as that Young Man, if they Wanted to be, and if their Parents Wanted to Produce all such Beautiful People. Indeed, they would only have to Learn HOW and WHY, which all Good Doctors would be Happy to Teach them, including myself. [_] If you Agree, please Check the Box with the Appropriate Color.}

— Chapter 40 —

A Long List of other Fascinating Literature by the same Inspired Author

[_] 40-001 — "LIGHTNING **Versus the** Lightning Bug!" (HOW almost Everyone can become Moderately RICH, without Telling Any Lies nor Selling Any Capitalist Trash!) By The Worldwide People's Revolution!® Book 001B.

[_] 40-002 — "What is WRong with those Professing Christians?" (A Self-Examination of the Heart of the Body of Good Government!) By The Worldwide People's Revolution!® Book 002B.

[_] 40-003 — "For the Love of Money!" (The Strange Things that People Say and Do to Get more Money!) By The Worldwide People's Revolution!® Book 003B.

[_] 40-004 — "How Best to Prepare for CLIMATE CHANGES!" (The Wisest Plan for Mankind to Follow!) By The Worldwide People's Revolution!® Book 004B.

[_] 40-005 — "Why do I have to be Surrounded by CRAZY PEOPLE!" (Do almost all People Feel like they are Surrounded by CRAZY People?) By The Worldwide People's Revolution!® Book 005B.

[_] 40-006 — "The Washington Journal is a FARCE! (C-SPAN Managers are not very WISE!) By The Worldwide People's Revolution!® Book 006C. (This Book has lots of Good Humor.)

[_] 40-007 — "The PRAYERS of PUMPKINHEADS!" (This Book is otherwise known as the Prayers of Preachers, Priests, Professors, Politicians, Prostitutes, Policemen, Pumpkinheads, Punks, Prisoners, and other Professionals — in other Words, the Capital P People!) By The Worldwide People's Revolution!® Book 007B. (Some of it is for Adults only.)

[_] 40-008 — "A Sound Argument for Good Masters and Obedient Servants!" (WHY Everyone Needs a Good Master, and every

Master Needs Good Obedient Servants!) By The Worldwide People's Revolution!® Book 008B.

[_] 40-009 — "WHY are some Preachers so POOR?" (HOW almost all Preachers can Get Moderately RICH, without Preaching any Outlandish LIES!) By The Worldwide People's Revolution!® Book 009B.

[_] 40-010 — "GOOD NEWS for REBEL WOMEN!" (HOW almost all Wives can become Moderately RICH without Leaving their Homes! Guaranteed!) By The Worldwide People's Revolution!® Book 010B.

[_] 40-011 — "The Low Court of Supreme Injustices is Brought to Trial!" (Our Selected King Butts Heads with the United States Supreme Court, with or without their Black Robes of Hypocrisies and Lies!) By The Worldwide People's Revolution!® Book 011B. (This Inspired Book contains the Famous *Declaration of Interdependence,* which is a Must Read. It also contains the Correct Wording for the Placard on the Statue of Liberty.)

[_] 40-012 — "The Right Design for Living!" (A List of Great Advantages for Building Beautiful Planned City States!) By The Worldwide People's Revolution!® Book 012B. (This Book contains many Important Drawings, as well as HOW to Save hundreds of Trillions of Dollars by Building Swanky Fortresses, and Living in Peace within them. It is a Companion Book of Book 011B, which contains many more Great Advantages for Swanky Fortresses.)

[_] 40-013 — **"The Gospel According to The Worldwide People's Revolution!®" (The Good News from the Most Modern Perspective!)** See Book 077. (This Book contains the Famous Sermon of Jonah to the Ninevites, whereby 120,000 People Repented in Sackcloth and Ashes! Do not Miss Out on it. Not even the Rev. Dr. Billy Graham got 120,000 Converts during one Day!)

[_] 40-014 — **"Poverty Hunger Riots Strikes Police Brutalities Election Deceptions and Civil Wars!" (The High Price that we Earthlings have Paid for Leaving the Good Land!)** By The Worldwide People's Revolution!® Book 014B.

[_] 40-015 — **"Seven Great Armies of Working Soldiers!" (HOW to Provide a Way for Everyone to WORK: so as to Eliminate Poverty,**

Crimes, Drug Abuses, Prisons and Unnecessary Taxes!) By The Worldwide People's Revolution!® Book 015B. (This Book contains a True-Life Story when the Author was in the Army.)

[_] 40-016 — "The CONSTITUTION for the New RIGHTEOUS One-World Government!" (HOW all Peoples can get True Justice, and Celebrate the Great Year of JUBILEE!) By The Worldwide People's Revolution!® Book 016B.

[_] 40-017 — "The Great World TEMPLE of PEACE!" (The Glory of Jerusalem Arises Again in the Great State of Flexible Texas!) By The Worldwide People's Revolution!® Book 017B.

[_] 40-018 — "The Swanky Associations of Working Soldiers!" (A Fascinating Collection of Various Kinds of Voluntary Working Soldiers!) By The Worldwide People's Revolution!® Book 018B. (There will be thousands of Associations for all Kinds of Occupations, which will Specialize in Fine Arts — such as Hand-carved Leather-bound Books. See "LIGHTNING STRIKES Versus Lightning Bugs!" (HOW you can Become Moderately RICH, without Telling any Lies nor Selling any Trash!) By The Worldwide People's Revolution!® Book 074, for a Picture of a Good Example.)

[_] 40-019 — "GLORIOUS Swanky Hotels Castles and Fortresses!" (Beautiful Planned City States for WISE Intelligent Well-Educated People with Common Sense and Good Understanding!) By The Worldwide People's Revolution!® Book 019B. (This Book contains many Rough Drawings, which could be Greatly Improved upon by someone who Knows the Art, and has the Correct Computer Programs for doing it.)

[_] 40-020 — "Are you a Jobless Graduate of the SKQL uv FQLZ?" (HOW to Get a GOUD EJUKAASHUN without Robbing the Bank!) By The Worldwide People's Revolution!® Book 020B. (This Inspired Book contains the New MAGNIFIED Version {NMV} of *First Corinthians 13*, plus: HOW to Produce Pure Living Water!)

[_] 40-021 — "The LUSCIOUS All-Mineral Organic Method of Gardening!" (HOW to Grow DELICIOUS Satisfying Foods for Potential Kingz and Kweenz in Beautiful Swanky PALACES!) By The Worldwide People's Revolution!® Book 021B. (This Book Explains HOW to make a Flood-proof Garden, while Trapping the Rainwater.)

[_] 40-022 — "Did God or Satan Ordain Medical Doctors?" (Ask Huck Finn and/or Nigger Jim: because neither Tom Sawyer nor Judge Thatcher would Know!) By The Worldwide People's Revolution!® Book 022B. (This Inspired Book Reveals HOW to Prevent Common Colds, and has a Special Chapter that Explains what a True "Nigger" IS. Surprise yourself!)

[_] 40-023 — "The BIG White OUTHOUSE on the Not-so-Biblical Capitol DUNGHILL!" (The Chief Sins of the Divided States of United Lies!) By The Worldwide People's Revolution!® Book 023B. (This Book contains Special Words that most People have never Heard! Surprise yourself again!)

[_] 40-024 — "The Public School of IGNERUNT FQLZ!" (HOW we have been GRAATLEE DISEEVD by Capitalism!) By The Worldwide People's Revolution!® Book 024B. (This Book Teaches Children HOW to "Reed and Riit in Funetik Ingglish in just wun Daa!" You should Challenge your Frendz and Naaberz with it.)

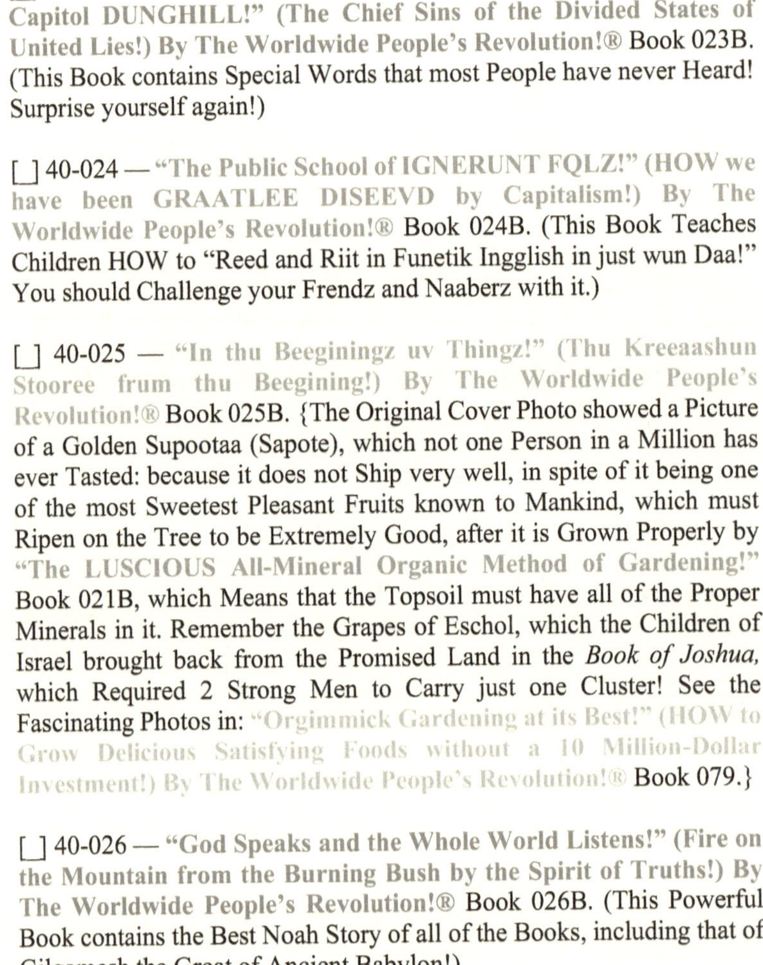

[_] 40-025 — "In thu Beeginingz uv Thingz!" (Thu Kreeaashun Stooree frum thu Beegining!) By The Worldwide People's Revolution!® Book 025B. {The Original Cover Photo showed a Picture of a Golden Supootaa (Sapote), which not one Person in a Million has ever Tasted: because it does not Ship very well, in spite of it being one of the most Sweetest Pleasant Fruits known to Mankind, which must Ripen on the Tree to be Extremely Good, after it is Grown Properly by "The LUSCIOUS All-Mineral Organic Method of Gardening!" Book 021B, which Means that the Topsoil must have all of the Proper Minerals in it. Remember the Grapes of Eschol, which the Children of Israel brought back from the Promised Land in the *Book of Joshua,* which Required 2 Strong Men to Carry just one Cluster! See the Fascinating Photos in: "Orgimmick Gardening at its Best!" (HOW to Grow Delicious Satisfying Foods without a 10 Million-Dollar Investment!) By The Worldwide People's Revolution!® Book 079.}

[_] 40-026 — "God Speaks and the Whole World Listens!" (Fire on the Mountain from the Burning Bush by the Spirit of Truths!) By The Worldwide People's Revolution!® Book 026B. (This Powerful Book contains the Best Noah Story of all of the Books, including that of Gilgamesh the Great of Ancient Babylon!)

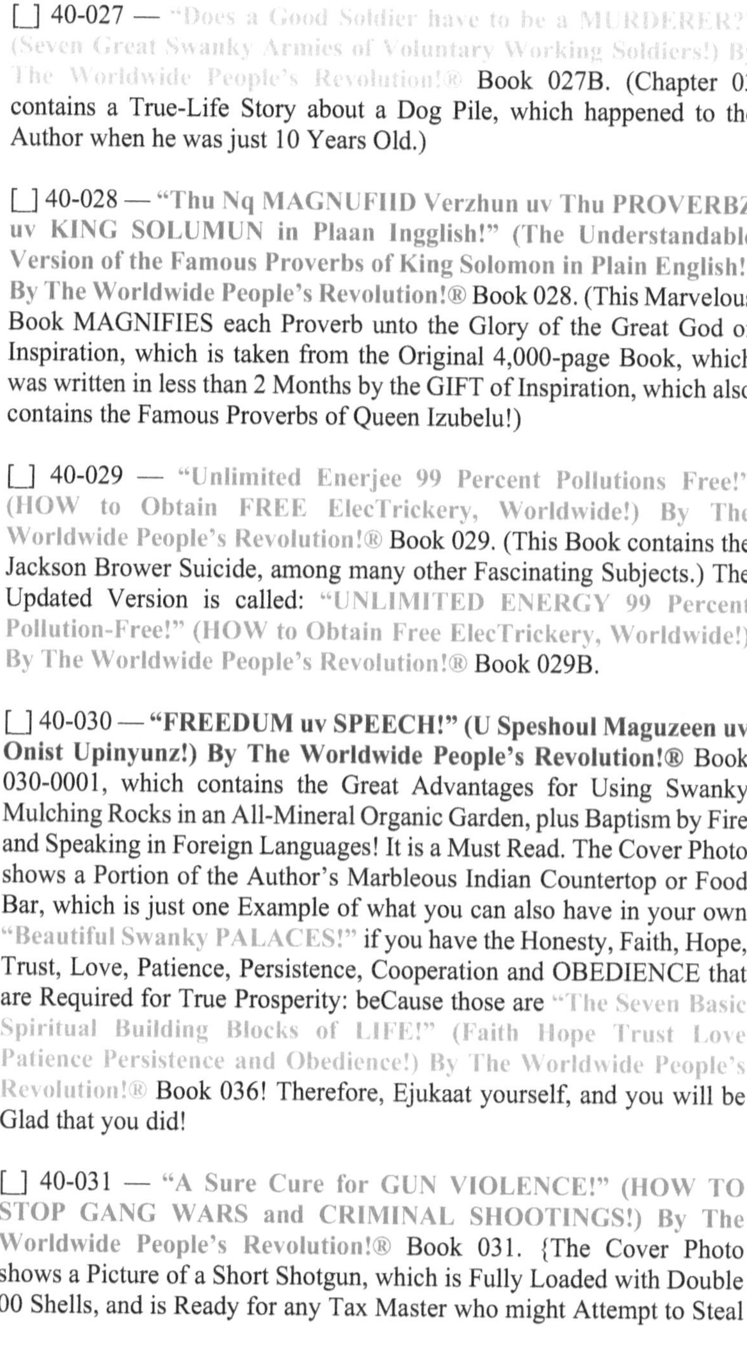

[_] 40-027 — "Does a Good Soldier have to be a MURDERER?" (Seven Great Swanky Armies of Voluntary Working Soldiers!) By The Worldwide People's Revolution!® Book 027B. (Chapter 03 contains a True-Life Story about a Dog Pile, which happened to the Author when he was just 10 Years Old.)

[_] 40-028 — "Thu Nq MAGNUFIID Verzhun uv Thu PROVERBZ uv KING SOLUMUN in Plaan Ingglish!" (The Understandable Version of the Famous Proverbs of King Solomon in Plain English!) By The Worldwide People's Revolution!® Book 028. (This Marvelous Book MAGNIFIES each Proverb unto the Glory of the Great God of Inspiration, which is taken from the Original 4,000-page Book, which was written in less than 2 Months by the GIFT of Inspiration, which also contains the Famous Proverbs of Queen Izubelu!)

[_] 40-029 — "Unlimited Enerjee 99 Percent Pollutions Free!" (HOW to Obtain FREE ElecTrickery, Worldwide!) By The Worldwide People's Revolution!® Book 029. (This Book contains the Jackson Brower Suicide, among many other Fascinating Subjects.) The Updated Version is called: "UNLIMITED ENERGY 99 Percent Pollution-Free!" (HOW to Obtain Free ElecTrickery, Worldwide!) By The Worldwide People's Revolution!® Book 029B.

[_] 40-030 — "FREEDUM uv SPEECH!" (U Speshoul Maguzeen uv Onist Upinyunz!) By The Worldwide People's Revolution!® Book 030-0001, which contains the Great Advantages for Using Swanky Mulching Rocks in an All-Mineral Organic Garden, plus Baptism by Fire and Speaking in Foreign Languages! It is a Must Read. The Cover Photo shows a Portion of the Author's Marbleous Indian Countertop or Food Bar, which is just one Example of what you can also have in your own "Beautiful Swanky PALACES!" if you have the Honesty, Faith, Hope, Trust, Love, Patience, Persistence, Cooperation and OBEDIENCE that are Required for True Prosperity: beCause those are "The Seven Basic Spiritual Building Blocks of LIFE!" (Faith Hope Trust Love Patience Persistence and Obedience!) By The Worldwide People's Revolution!® Book 036! Therefore, Ejukaat yourself, and you will be Glad that you did!

[_] 40-031 — "A Sure Cure for GUN VIOLENCE!" (HOW TO STOP GANG WARS and CRIMINAL SHOOTINGS!) By The Worldwide People's Revolution!® Book 031. {The Cover Photo shows a Picture of a Short Shotgun, which is Fully Loaded with Double 00 Shells, and is Ready for any Tax Master who might Attempt to Steal the Retirement Home, who never moved a Finger to Help Build the Rock Houses, whereby we moved more than 66,666,666 Pounds by Hand, whose Property was Cunningly Stolen by that False Anti-Christ WICKED Cover-up Government, which allowed Bankers to Rob us of 30 Years of Hard Labor and more than 300,000 dollars-worth of Investments in our Uncommon American Farm, which is Explained in: "LIGHTNING STRIKES Versus Lightning Bugs!" (HOW you can Become Moderately RICH, without Telling any Lies nor Selling any Trash!) By The Worldwide People's Revolution!® Book 074, which contains many Photographs with Profound Explanations! Do not be left out in the Darkness of Ignorance. Get Informed, now: beCause, **"The Great False Economy is now DEBUNKED!"** Book 053.}

[ ] 40-032 — "AIIRMWVC and Reasonable Solutions!" (Aliens, Illegal Immigrants, Refugees, Migrant Workers and other Victims of Capitalism!) By The Worldwide People's Revolution!® Book 032. (This Inspired Book contains *the New MAGNIFIED Version of Job 33*.)

[ ] 40-033 — "MARK TWAIN Races for the PRESIDENCY with a Landslide VICTORY!" (The 2020 Presidential Candidates Desperately Need Some STRONG Undefeatable COMPETITION!) By The Worldwide People's Revolution!® Book 033B. {This Book contains a Part of the Author's Autobiography, and his Personal Answers to the Questions in: "The Complete SURVEYS of our VALUES!" (SURVEYS of Religious Spiritual Political Governmental Sexual Social Moral Economic Business Labor Habitual and Miscellaneous VALUES!) Book 059. **The CONDENSED Version is Book 033C,** which most People Prefer.}

[ ] 40-034 — "ECCLESIASTES Uncovered and Recovered!" (The New MAGNIFIED Version of Ecclesiastes and the Song of Solomon in Plain English!) By The Worldwide People's Revolution!® Book 034. (This is the Book that contains the Famous Sayings for *"There is a Time to be Born, and a Time to Die ..."* which has been Greatly Magnified!)

[ ] 40-035 — "The Environmentalists' Perfect Paradise!" (HOW almost Everyone can be Living in a Beautiful Manmade Paradise!) By The Worldwide People's Revolution!® Book 035C. (This Book contains the NMV of *Psalm 48,* which will Amaze you, O Lady Doubtfulness!)

[ ] 40-036 — "The Seven Basic Spiritual Building Blocks of LIFE!" (Faith Hope Trust Love Patience Persistence and Obedience!) By The Worldwide People's Revolution!® Book 036. (This Book contains the Mockingbird's Version of *Hebrews 11,* plus the NMV of *First Corinthians 13,* among many other "Goodies.")

[ ] 40-037 — "DIETS!" (A Reasonable Solution for the "Eternal Controversy"!) By The Worldwide People's Revolution!® Book 037.

[ ] 40-038 — "The Nature of CAPITALISM!" (A List of the EVILS of CAPITALISM!) By The Worldwide People's Revolution!® Book 038.

[ ] 40-039 — "SWANGKEENOMIKS Rules the Roost!" (HOW all People can Prosper in a RIIT WAA, and STOP Polluting the Earth with Capitalist TRASH!) By The Worldwide People's Revolution!® Book 039. (The Cover Photo shows a Portion of the Author's Retirement Home, before the 5,000+ square-feet Concrete Roof was Installed, after moving more than 66 Million Pounds by Hand, and mostly by his own Boastful Hands!)

[ ] 40-040 — "The New MAGNIFIED Version of The Book of MORMON!" (The Story of the White and Dark Indians in the Americas!) By Big Chief Standsover Bull in River of Life! Book 040, which comes in 2 Volumes of about 500 Pages, each. The Cover Photo on the First Volume shows the Queen of England's Golden Coach, and the Cover Photo on the Second Volume shows one of many Polished Spanish Marble Walls in our Selected King's Retirement Home, which is worth a thousand dollars per square yard, which is another Example of what you can also have, if you simply OBEY your Righteous KING! All such Marble is very Inspiring. No one could Study it for very long without Believing in a Great Creator God. The Picture does not do it Justice. You would have to See it in Person, and Wash it with Pure Water to bring Out the Beauty of it.

[ ] 40-041 — "The GREAT Worldwide TELEVISED Court HEARING!" (That Great Meeting of the Most-Intelligent and Well-Educated Minds!) By The Worldwide People's Revolution!® Book 041B. {This is the Book that the World has long been Waiting for: beCause it will Overthrow the Evil Empires, and make it Possible to Establish "The New RIGHTEOUS One-World Government!" (HOW to Establish a Righteous One-World Government without Going to WAR!) By The Worldwide People's Revolution!® Book

131

056. This is the Greatest Idea since the Invention of the Light Bulb, Guaranteed!}

[_] 40-042 — **"The Secret City of the Great King!"** (HOW the True Church will Escape from the Great Tribulation!) By **The Worldwide People's Revolution!®** Book 042. (Be Sure to Inform your Friends, Relatives and Naaberz about this Wonderful Book: beCause they might also Want to Escape!)

[_] 40-043 — **"Terrorists Beware that your Days are Numbered!"** (HOW to Bring those Terrorist Attacks to a Screeching HALT!) By The Worldwide People's Revolution!® Book 043. (This Book also contains the Fascinating Book of LEHI, which has now been Restored!) †‡

[_] 40-044 — **"The New MAGNIFIED Version of ISAIAH in Plain English!"** (The Understandable Version of the Book of Isaiah!) By The Worldwide People's Revolution!® Book 044. (The Cover Photo shows a Swanky Potato and Avocado Salad with Sweet Peas and Corn, among other "Secret" Ingredients, which are Revealed within the Book. Remember that you can read many Words for Free in the Book Previews on www.Amazon.com.usa or UK.)

[_] 40-045 — **"HOW to Become a HOLY Man!"** (40 Good Reasons WHY People Should FAST and PRAY!) By The Worldwide People's Revolution!® Book 045, which is a Companion Book of:

[_] 40-046 — **"The Proper RULES for FASTING!"** (The Complete Instruction Manual for True Repentance!) By The Worldwide People's Revolution!® Book 046, which is a Companion Book of the above-mentioned Book, which contains a True-Life Story about an Old Black Mare called Lucy, who Fasted for 30 Days without Food nor Water, who was Physiologically "Born Again," as Jesus might say. See the Full Details in: "The New MAGNIFIED Version of The GOOD NEWS According to Saint JOHN!" (The Gospel According to Saint John Zebedee Boanerges in Plain English!) Book 062, which contains many Inspiring Photographs with Explanations!

[_] 40-047 — **"Are Americans the Most-STUPID People who ever Lived?"** (HOW Working People can PROSPER and Live in PEACE Under the Rulership of a RIGHTEOUS KING!) By The Worldwide People's Revolution!® Book 047. (The Cover Photo shows a large Portion of the Author's Living Room Floor, which is worth 100,000$, which is just another Good Example of what you can also have, just for Loving and Obeying your Elected King!)

[_] 40-048 — "An Amazing Collection of Wit and Wisdom!" (The Marvelous Tale of the Colorful Peacock from Angel Ridge, and the Strong Rope of Everlasting Hope!) By The Worldwide People's Revolution!® Book 048. (The Cover Photo shows a Book Display, which will be Greatly Enhanced during the Future, when all 364+ Inspired Books are on Display in a Swanky Truth-brary, as Opposed to the Public LIE-brary.)

[_] 40-049 — "Justifications for Capitalizations!" (WHY our Selected King DEFIES the School of FOOLS by Capitalizing LOVE and HATE!) By The Worldwide People's Revolution!® Book 049.

[_] 40-050 — "The END of CONFUSION!" (The Great CELEBRATION of the Magnificent Wedding of the Most-Humble, Honest Nations, and the Grand Year of JUBILEE!) By The Worldwide People's Revolution!® Book 050. (Just Try to Visualize those **"Seven Great Swanky Armies of Voluntary Working Soldiers"** Marching through the Valley of Megiddo, being Dressed in their Colorful Robes, while the Band Plays *The Battle Hymn of the Republic,* and the Choirs Sing the Praises of the Great KING of Kings! What a Sight and Sound that will be, which will be Climaxed in "The Great World TEMPLE of PEACE," when the Nations will get Married, along with our Elected King! Come one, come all to "The GREAT Worldwide TELEVISED Court HEARING," by Means of your Wide Flat-screen TVs, whereby you might Learn WHY, WHEN and HOW!) †‡

[_] 40-051 — "The Loathsome Burdens of the Independent Jackasses!" (A New Civilized Approach for Quietly Solving our Massive Problems!) By The Worldwide People's Revolution!® Book 051. (Just Think about the Multitude of almost Worthless Meetings of the Minds, who Strained themselves to Think of Reasonable Solutions for our Massive Problems, who sometimes even Prayed to God for Help; but, the Best Solutions have been here for no less than 40 Years — Thanks to the Spirit of Inspiration from GOD!)

[_] 40-052 — "Are we Tax Slaves of a Lower Order than those Lying Conniving EDOMITES!" (HOW to be Liberated From all Forms of Slavery, Worldwide!) By The Worldwide People's Revolution!® Book 052B. {This Inspired Book once had another Title and Author, which was not Acceptable by Amazon, which has now been Restored in all of its Glory, and is Published by more Trustworthy People, who are not Afraid of Controversies, nor of: "The Swanky Sword of Divine Truths!" (The Most-Powerful Weapon in the Whole Universe!) By The Worldwide People's Revolution!® Book 067.}

[_] 40-053 — "The Great False Economy is now DEBUNKED!" (Adolf Hitler had a much Better Economic System!) By The Worldwide People's Revolution!® Book 053. {Trust me, Adolf was no Saint; but, during the Day of God's Judgment, he will be Justified, while his Anti-Christ Opponents will be Condemned: beCause they Refused to Attend a Worldwide Radio Debate with Adolf Hitler, whose Arguments will Stand Up during the Day of Judgment, which would have Prevented World War 2, and thus Saved the Lives of no less than 60 Million People! Likewise, we Tax Slaves must now Act more Wisely, and DEMAND "The GREAT Worldwide TELEVISED Court HEARING," Book 041B, whereby we might Save the World from that Dreadful Battle of Megiddo, called *Armageddon!* Yes, the Ball is now in YOUR Hands, O Potential Friend or Enemy, and you are now Responsible for it. Therefore, do not Shirk your Duty as a Free Citizen; but, Help us to Spread this Message, far and wide, whereby the Masses of People will be Demanding The GWTCH, and thus, Prevent "The Great ATOMIC NIGHTMARE!" (The Saddest Story in World History!) By The Great White Bald Eagle! Book 099.}

[_] 40-054 — "The UGLY Scarred Dishonest Face of Poor Old Miserable UNCLE SAM!" (A Memorial Day Legacy!) By The Worldwide People's Revolution!® Book 054. {NOTE: This Inspired Book was also Suppressed by Amazon, who will be most Ashamed of themselves if they do not Un-suppress it during the Future: beCause it will also be Published by People of Greater Faith, who Know for a Fact that it is the TRUTH! Therefore, just be Patient. Search for Book 054B, *King James Version.*}

[_] 40-055 — "The United States of the Whole World!" (A True Global Economy for the Masses of Working People!) By The Worldwide People's Revolution!® Book 055. (This Inspired Book contains many Colored Photographs with Explanations. It is a Good Book to Publish in Foreign Nations, who are not so Blinded by their Pride, who can See the Mountain of Lies much Better at a Distance from them: beCause of not being a Part of the American Corruption.) †‡

[_] 40-056 — "The New RIGHTEOUS One-World Government!" (HOW to Establish a Righteous One-World Government without Going to WAR!) By The Worldwide People's Revolution!® Book 056. (This is a KEY Book, which everyone should Study Carefully and Prayerfully.)

[_] 40-057 — "The Many Ridiculous Contradictions within the Holy Bible!" (HOW to Read the Mutilated Bible with an Honest Open Mind!) By The Worldwide People's Revolution!® Book 057. {NOTE: Many Professing "Christians" Falsely Claim that their so-called *"Holy Bibles"* do not Contain any Contradictions, being "the Infallible Inspired Word of the Living God," but, without the Capitalized Words, and without Explaining just WHY there are more than 200 Contradictory Versions of it! This Book Reveals how to Deal with those Biblical Problems, and come to Understand WHY God Allowed it to Happen for the Truth's Sake. Trust God: beCause, you have never Heard this Explanation before now. See also: "C-SPAN-DEX!" (Your Filtered View of Bad Government!) By The Worldwide People's Revolution!® Book 097.}

[_] 40-058 — "The Divided States of United Lies!" (The so-called "United States of North America" in Disguise!) By The Worldwide People's Revolution!® Book 058. {NOTE: This is perhaps the most Referred to Book among all of the Books by our Selected King; but, that does not Mean that it is his Best Book by any Means, which is Well Camouflaged: so that it will Survive the Test of Time, even if the others are BURNED by the Anti-Christ Followers of Satan, who are Possession Worshipers of the Worst Kind, who Seek to Justify American Lies, rather than Quickly Confess them, and thus Escape from their Self-made Prison of Propagandish Lies! Just be Perfectly Honest, and you will have no Problem with any of our Literature.}

[_] 40-059 — "The Complete SURVEYS of our VALUES!" (SURVEYS of Religious Spiritual Political Governmental Sexual Social Moral Economical Business Labor Habitual and Miscellaneous VALUES!) By The Worldwide People's Revolution!® Book 059. {NOTE: According to our Selected King, every Potential Leader in the World must Fill Out and File those Surveys on the Internet for everyone to Study, whereby the Best People might be Elected by those Wise People who have also Filled Out the Simplistic Surveys of their own Values, whereby they will be Qualified to VOTE. Otherwise, they will not be Qualified to Vote, which will Eliminate a LOT of Wasted Money on Election Deceptions, while at the same Time it will Educate a lot of Ignorant People, who Desperately Need to Study that Inspired Book before Voting for another Dimwitcrat, Reprobate, or Independent Jackass!}

[_] 40-059B — "The Simplistic SURVEYS of our VALUES!" Book 059B. (The Cover Photo shows some Beautiful African Antelopes, who are Free with a Capital F.)

[_] 40-060 — "HOW to Get our PRIORITIES in ORDER!" (The Glories of Democracy; and, Does DEMON-ocracy have its Priorities in Order?) By The Worldwide People's Revolution!® Book 060. This Book will need to be Re-written by a Collective Group of Wise People, who will Contribute their True-Life Stories during the Future, when they Wake Up and come to their Right Senses with the Prodigal Son of *Luke 15*. See:

[_] 40-061 — "The New MAGNIFIED Version of The GOOD NEWS According to Saint LUKE!" (The Magnified Gospel of Saint Luke in Plain English!) By The Worldwide People's Revolution!® Book 061, which is by Far the Best Version of that Gospel on the Earth, which has no Rivals at all among the other 200+ Versions. Guaranteed!

[_] 40-062 — "The New MAGNIFIED Version of The GOOD NEWS According to Saint JOHN!" (The Gospel According to Saint John Zebedee Boanerges [pronounced Boo-an-er-jeez] in Plain English!) By The Worldwide People's Revolution!® Book 062, which also has no Rivals among all of the other Versions: beCause this is no Translation of anything; but, it is the Inspired Words of the Living God, which were Revealed by the Holy Spirit to our Selected King, who has not Died, yet.

[_] 40-063 — "The New MAGNIFIED Version of the Book of ACTS!" (The Understandable Version of the Acts of the Apostles in Plain English!) By The Worldwide People's Revolution!® Book 063. (This Inspired Book makes it Understandable WHY the Jews Hated the Apostles so much. You will have to Read it to Believe it.)

[_] 40-064 — "The New MAGNIFIED Version of the PSALMS of King David!" (The Understandable Version of the Famous Psalms in Plain English!) By The Worldwide People's Revolution!® Book 064. You will be Amazed!

[_] 40-065 — "A List of FAIR Swanky Wages!" (The Equitable Wage System!) By The Worldwide People's Revolution!® Book 065.

(All Hardworking People will LOVE this Good Book! You will also, if you Study it Carefully.)

[ ] 40-066 — "Beautiful Swanky PALACES!" (A New Concept in Living Habits — Swanky Palaces for Poor People!) By The Worldwide People's Revolution!® Book 066. (You have no Idea what a "Swanky Palace" IS, unless you have read this Unique Book, or another one that Describes those Palaces, and several of them do; but, this one has the Best Description. ENJOY!)

[ ] 40-067 — "The Swanky Sword of Divine Truths!" (The Most-Powerful Weapon in the Whole Universe!) By The Worldwide People's Revolution!® Book 067. (The very Reason that our Selected King has no Rivals is beCause of the Swanky Sword of Divine Truths, which no one can Defeat by any Means. Therefore, you Need to have it on your own Side, whereby no one can Defeat your Arguments! Be Strong, be Brave, have Faith and put on the Whole Armor of GOD!)

[ ] 40-068 — "Has your Life become Extremely Complicated?" (HOW to Live a SIMPLE Life!) By The Worldwide People's Revolution!® Book 068. (Many People are not even Aware of just how Complicated their Lives are, until suddenly they are ready to Commit Suicide! It is Best to Prevent all such Evil Things, and this Book tells HOW.)

[ ] 40-069 — "The IDEAL Place to Live!" (HOW to Discover the Ideal Place to Live!) By The Worldwide People's Revolution!® Book 069. {NOTE: Our Selected King Searched the World over, and did not Discover any Idea Place to Live. Therefore, he Concluded that we must Make our own. Yes, we must Build those "GLORIOUS Swanky Hotels Castles and Fortresses!" (Beautiful Planned City States for WISE Intelligent Well-Educated People with Common Sense and Good Understanding!) By The Worldwide People's Revolution!® Book 019B, even if we must DRAFT "Seven Great Armies of Working Soldiers!" (HOW to Provide a Way for Everyone to WORK: so as to Eliminate Poverty, Crimes, Drug Abuses, Prisons and Unnecessary Taxes!) By The Worldwide People's Revolution!® Book 015B; and what on this Good Earth could Prove to be more Profitable than that, and without going to WAR?}

[ ] 40-070 — "Our Elected King Who Speaks Out!" (It is High Time for some Sane Person to Get Control of this Insane World!) By The Worldwide People's Revolution!® Book 070. (This Inspired Book

contains a Special Speech that is Addressed to both Houses of the Congress in Washington. You will Love it, O Honest Man of Greater Faith!)

[_] 40-071 — **"How GAY is GOD?" (Oh, the Wonders of it all, when it ALL Hangs Out!) By The Worldwide People's Revolution!® Book** 071. (Do not Judge the Book, until you have Carefully "Red" all of it. You will be Surprised by the Provable Truths within it, and Greatly Humored by the Author's Exceptionally Good Humor, who is less Gay than God, who has never had any Sexual Intercourse during his entire Life! In other Words, he is a VIRGIN!)

[_] 40-072 — **"LIGHTNING STRIKES Versus Lightning Bugs and Impotent Fireflies!" (A Memorial Photo Album of some Real American Heroes!) By The Worldwide People's Revolution!® Book** 072. (NOTE: This Book is Unique among all of the Books by our Selected King: beCause he did not get to Proof-read it before the Computer Crashed. It just Happened to be Saved on a Computer Chip before the Computer Crashed, and therefore it was Saved in PDF. But, the Corrections did not get made, which makes it a Special Collector's Item, which has more than 100 Colored Photos, which was what Caused the Crash.) †‡

[_] 40-073 — **"The BEST of CAPITALISM!" (Corrections for: "LIGHTNING STRIKES Versus Lightning Bugs and Impotent Fireflies!")** Book 073. (It is a completely new Book, except for those Corrections; and it is one of the Best Books in the World, which all Honest People will Love.)

[_] 40-074 — **"LIGHTNING STRIKES Versus Lightning Bugs!" (HOW you can Become Moderately RICH, without Telling any Lies nor Selling any Trash!) By The Worldwide People's Revolution!®** Book 074, which is the Perfection of all of the Lightning Striking Books, which is Recommended above all others for Mass Production: beCause it stands the Best Chance of being a Real Winner, just after this Book that you are now Reading, which has a Magnetizing Title!

[_] 40-075 — **"What are the PUNISHMENTS for Dietary Sins?" (Have we Served ourselves Well at the Tables of our Lusts?) By The Worldwide People's Revolution!®** Book 075. (This Book is too Controversial to be Published at this Time. Be very Patient until it is Available: beCause it is HOT!)

[_] 40-076 — "What is WRong with those CRAZY CHRISTIANS?" (A Self-Examination of the Heart of the Body of Good Government!) By The Worldwide People's Revolution!® Book 076.

[_] 40-077 — "The Gospel According to our Elected King!" (The Good News from the Most Modern Perspective!) By The Worldwide People's Revolution!® Book 077. (This is perhaps the Best Book that you will Discover on Amazon, which contains the Famous Sermon that Jonah gave to the Ninevites, plus a very Special Sermon by Jesus Christ, himself, which is taken from the Dead Sea Scrolls! It is simply a Marvelous Book that everyone must "Reed." ENJOY!) ‡

[_] 40-078 — "The Root Cause for almost all Evils!" (The Strange Things that People Say and Do to Get more Money!) By The Worldwide People's Revolution!® Book 078. (This Book contains many Colored Photographs with Fascinating Explanations!)

[_] 40-079 — "Orgimmick Gardening at its Best!" (HOW to Grow Delicious Satisfying Foods without a 10 Million-Dollar Investment!) By The Worldwide People's Revolution!® Book 079. (This Book also contains many Colored Photographs with Wonderful Explanations!)

[_] 40-080 — "Guaranteed Solutions!" (HOW to Solve our Local and Global Problems in the Most-Rational Manner Possible!) By The Worldwide People's Revolution!® Book 080. (See the Description on Amazon: because they Offer a ONE-MILLION-DOLLAR REWARD to anyone who can Prove our Selected King's Solutions to be WRong or Unworkable! Can you Beat that? Do you have all such Guaranteed Solutions? Does any Politician? Only our Selected King has those Provable Solutions: beCause God Blest him with them, which can be Proven in any Courtroom with Law and Order. ENJOY!)

[_] 40-081 — "Mexicans are more Intelligent than Americans!" (A Unique Challenge to all Americans and Mexicans!) By The Worldwide People's Revolution!® Book 081. {NOTE: The Remaining 275 Inspired Books by the Author of this Book may only be found in English, until we can get them Properly Translated into other Languages. Shame on you People who Killed him, who Broke his Heart with your Unbelief. May God have Mercy on your Poor Wretched Souls.} †§‡

[_] 40-081B — "¡Los Mexicanos son más Inteligentes que los Estadounidenses!" (¡Un Desafío Único para todos los Estadounidenses y Mexicanos!) By The Worldwide People's

Revolution!® Book 082. {NOTA: Aquí está el primer Libro en Español, que puede no ser Perfecto; pero, es Perfectamente lo Suficientemente Bueno para Iluminar las Mentes de quien lo Estudia.}

[_] 40-082 — **"The Process of Making a RIGHTEOUS KING!" (A Fascinating Autobiography of our Selected King!) By The Worldwide People's Revolution!®** Book 082. {NOTE: He once had a 6,000-plus-page Autobiography, called: **"DIARRHEA of the Mind!"** which gave Details of his entire Life, since he was only 4 Years Old, when he had an Encounter with God, which has been Lost: beCause those Backup Disks became Obsolete, and were thus Trashed, along with the Obsolete Computer, which Costed 4,000-plus Dollars, along with the Hewlett-Packard Printer, which Costed another 4,000-plus Dollars, whose Antiquated Software would not Work with a Modern Computer, nor did Hewlett have an Updated Software Program for it: beCause they are Capitalist Scammers, who should be put Out of Business for Practicing Donald Trump Tactics! See: *"The Nature of CAPITALISM!" (A List of the EVILS of CAPITALISM!) By The Worldwide People's Revolution!®* Book 038.}

[_] 40-083 — **"Was Billy Graham Greatly Deceived?" (Giving Honor to whom Honor is Due!) By The Worldwide People's Revolution!®** Book 083. {NOTE: If you know a Grahamite, please Direct him or her to this Inspired Book, whereby he or she might be Converted to the Truths within it, and thus be Saved from Grahamite Perversions. Thank you in Advance. They will also Thank you for it: beCause they Suffer so Needlessly, when they should be Free, Healthy and Happy, like our Selected King, who has no Aches nor Pains, who used to Work Hard all Day long, and not be Weary, just like you can Reed in *the Book of Isaiah 40:31, NMV!*}

[_] 40-084 — **"The New MAGNIFIED Version of the Book of DEUTERONOMY!" (The Understandable Version of Deuteronomy in Plain English!)** Book 084. This is actually one of the Best Books within the entire Holy Bible, and also one of the Longest; but, do not allow that Fact to Deter you by any Means: beCause, "the Bigger Book is Normally a Better Book," which is True of a lot of Books, including all of the above Books: beCause it is the Nature of the Holy Spirit to get into Long-winded Sermons, you might say, which is WHY the Apostle Paul Preached until Midnight in *the Book of Acts,* until some Boy went to Sleep and Fell from a Window and Killed himself, whom the Apostle Paul Raised Up from the Dead and went on Preaching until the Dawn of the Day! And it is NOT Jewish Mythology! †§‡§§ {See: "The New

MAGNIFIED Version of the Book of ACTS" for the Finest of Details, Book 063.}

[_] 40-085 — "All of the Arguments are in Favor of our Selected King, who has Zero Challengers!" (Before you Attend another Election Deception, you should Carefully Study this Inspired Book with an Honest Open Mind!) By The Worldwide People's Revolution!® Book 085.

[_] 40-086 — "Provable Truths that True Christians cannot Rightly Deny!" (A Fair Challenge for all Professing "Christians" to Meditate on with Honest Open Minds!) By The Worldwide People's Revolution!® Book 086.

[_] 40-087 — "How all Women can Get True Justice without Getting Divorced from God!" (The Unjust Case of Judge Brett Kavanaugh and Doctor Christine Blasey Ford is now Revisited by a Wise Son of King Solomon!) By The Worldwide People's Revolution!® B-087.

[_] 40-088 — "The New MAGNIFIED Version of GENESIS!" (The Enlightening Version of the Beginnings of Things!) By The Worldwide People's Revolution!® Book 088.

[_] 40-089 — "The New MAGNIFIED Version of the HOLY KORAN!" (WHY MuhamMAD went to Hell for Spiritual MURDER!) By The Worldwide People's Revolution!® Book 089. This is by Far the Best Version of the *Holy Koran,* which is Loved by all Honest Muslims, Hindus, Christians and Buddhists, Worldwide! Surprise yourself and others. Ask them what it Means? §‡

[_] 40-090 — "A New Jerusalem in the Great State of Flexible Texas!" (HOW to make Good Use of the Mississippi River!) By The Worldwide People's Revolution!® Book 090. This Book contains many Fascinating Photos of God's Handiwork. ENJOY!

[_] 40-091 — "What is The GREATEST SIN?" (And it is NOT Blasphemy Against the Holy Spirit!) By The Worldwide People's Revolution!® Book 091.

[_] 40-092 — "HOW to Make America (and all other Nations) Really GREAT Without Telling any LIES!" (The Founding Fathers would have Loved it!) By The Worldwide People's Revolution!® Book 092.

[_] 40-093 — "HOW Righteousness can Overcome Wickedness!" (The Triumph of the Soul who Knows God!) By The Enlightened Professor of Common Sense! Book 093. {Notice how the Calves in the Cover Photo Segregated themselves by their Colors, from Left to Right. God Guided them. ‡}

[_] 40-094 — "Justifications for MAGNIFICATIONS!" (The Problem with Understanding a Complicated Contradictory Mutilated Unholy Bible!) Or: (The Problem with Inventing Lies that are too BIG to DIE!) By The Worldwide People's Revolution!® Book 094.

[_] 40-095 — "HOW to IDENTIFY God's Elected Ones!" (Are YOU one of the Elect?) By The Worldwide People's Revolution!® Book 095.

[_] 40-096 — "GOVERNMENT Versus Independence!" (How Much CONTROL Should a Government Have?") By The Worldwide People's Revolution!® Book 096.

[_] 40-097 — "C-SPAN-DEX!" (Your Filtered View of Bad Government!) By The Worldwide People's Revolution!® Book 097.

[_] 40-098 — "Profitable Swanky MULCHING ROCKS!" (30 Advantages for Using Swanky Mulching Rocks in an All-Mineral Organic Garden!) By The Worldwide People's Revolution!® Book 098. {Just Think, the School of Fools never Mentioned them, nor did the False Government, nor any of the False Churches: beCause they are Uneducated and Foolish.}

[_] 40-099 — "The Great ATOMIC NIGHTMARE!" (The Saddest Story in World History!) By The Great White Bald Eagle! Book 099. {NOTE: Let us Hope and Pray that no one ever has to Write this Book; but, if they Do, it should Spook the Devil Out of you!}

[_] 40-100 — "Our Selected King SPEAKS OUT!" (It is High Time for some Sane Person to get Total Control of this Insane World!) By The Worldwide People's Revolution!® Book 100!

[_] 40-101 — "What will you Do when the Rain STOPS?" (God's Last Resort to Save Mankind from his MADNESS!) By The Worldwide People's Revolution!® Book 101!

[_]   40-102 — "Beautiful Swanky Stone Dome Home COMPLEXES!" (HOW to Build SECURE Tax-proof, Insurance-proof, Self-air-conditioned, Paint-proof, Rot-proof, Termite-proof, Mouse-proof, Fireproof, Tornado-proof, Hurricane-proof, Thief-proof, and BOMB-PROOF Houses!) By The Worldwide People's Revolution!® Book 102.

[_] 40-103 — "Royal Swanky Buffets!" (The Best Feasts in the Whole World!) By The Worldwide People's Revolution!® Book 103.

[_] 40-104 — "101 Good Reasons and Great Advantages for Establishing a Righteous One-World Government!" (Government By the People, Of the People, and For the People!) By The Worldwide People's Revolution!® Book 104. This Book Suggests thousands of Good Reasons and Great Advantages. But, of course, you have to be Able to THINK, which seems to be something that Wicked Politicians cannot Do, or Refuse to Do; and neither can most Preachers and Teachers Do it. Therefore, this Inspired Book will Help them to Think and Remember.

[_] 40-105 — "The New MAGNIFIED Version of the Book of REVELATION!" (The Understandable Version of the Most-Controversial Book in the Whole World!) By The Worldwide People's Revolution!® Book 105. This Proverbial "Bombshell" will be Published just before the Second Coming of Jesus Christ! Get your Seatbelts Fastened! Be Prepared for Radical Changes!

[_] 40-106 — "The Naked Glory of Beautiful Mankind!" (1,000 Pages of Sheer Artistic BEAUTY!) By The Worldwide People's Revolution!® Book 106. (See Book 014B-02-09-T for the Explanation.)

[_] 40-107 — "The Beautiful Faces of Holy Men!" (The very Best that God has to Offer!) By The Worldwide People's Revolution!® Book 107.

[_]   40-108 — "The Worldwide People's Revolution!" (A Comprehensive Plan for Obtaining Worldwide Law, Order, Obedience, Peace and True Prosperity!) By The Worldwide People's Revolution!® Book 108.

[_] 40-109 — "VOTE for The GOAT!" (The New Political Party that has Guaranteed Solutions for our Massive Problems!) By The Worldwide People's Revolution!® Book 109.

[_] 40-110 — "IMPORTANT THINGS that Should Have Been Written in the Holy Bible!" (A Special Challenge to all Professing Christians, Jews, Hindus, Muslims and Atheists!) **By The Irreverent Penname Scumbag! Book 110.**

[_] 40-111 — "Hosts of HOAXES Live In Under Around and Over the Little White OUTHOUSE!" (WHY Spiritually-Blind Cowardly-Americans are Hunkering Down in their Empty Root Cellars!) **By The Irreverent Penname Oversight! Book 111.**

[_] 40-112 — "Should Wives Obey their Husbands?" (OR, Should Husbands OBEY their Wives?) **By The Irreverent Penname Mockingbird! Book 112.**

[_] 40-113 — "Modern Deceived SLAVES!" (10 Simple Steps for Liberating ALL Modern Slaves, Worldwide, Including Yourself!) **By Liberty and Justice for ALL! Book 113.**

[_] 40-114 — "Are you a Jobless Graduate of the School of Fools?" (How to Obtain a Good Education without Robbing the Bank, Selling any Trash, nor Telling any Lies!) **By The Professor Wordcraft Enlightenment! Book 114.**

[_] 40-115 — "Beautiful Swanky FASTING SANITARIUMS!" (HOW to Learn Good Self-Discipline!) **By The Worldwide People's Revolution!® Book 115.**
[_] 40-116 — "Swanky Institutions for Compassionate Corrections!" (How to Correct even the Most-Stubborn Bullies!) **By The Biggest Bully of All Bullies! Book 116.**

[_] 40-117 — "What is True PROGRESS???" (Are we Making any True Progress, at all?) **By The Worldwide People's Revolution!® Book 117.**

[_] 40-118 — "Is America a White Nation with a Black Heart?" (How to Separate Truth from Fiction!) **By The Good Pastor of Uncommon Sense! Book 118.**

[_] 40-119 — "Which Church is the Right Church?" (Can all Churches be Correct?) **By The Good Pastor of Uncommon Sense! Book 119.**

[_] 40-120 — "Do People Go to Heaven when they Die?" (The Unbelievable Truth about Life and Death!) **By The Good Pastor of Uncommon Sense!** Book 120.

[_] 40-121 — "The Hopeless Church of Little Faith!" (The Unholy Church of Graceful Sinners, who are Mostly just Liars and Hypocrites!) **By The Good Pastor of Uncommon Sense!** Book 121.

[_] 40-122 — "HOW to Make Proper REPARATIONS!" (True Justice for Black and White People, and Everyone in Between them!) **By The Worldwide People's Revolution!®** Book 122. (This Book was Inspired by: https://youtu.be/QOPGpE-sXh0 The Truth about the Confederacy in the United States | Full Version.)

[_] 40-123 — "What would Moses and Jesus Do with the Statues and Monuments???" (A Unique Plan for Solving the Problem, which Everyone can be Extra Happy with!) **By Liberty and Justice is for ALL!** Book 123.

[_] 40-124 — "Belgiculture!" (A Complete Master Plan for Solving the Countless Problems of Mankind!) **By The Worldwide People's Revolution!®** Belgique Book 124.

[_] 40-125 — "Good Lessons for Honest Wise Men!" (A Simplistic Plan for Totally Solving the Complicated Problems of Deceived Mankind!) **By The Smarter Professor of Common Sense!** Book 125.

[_] 40-126 — "The Sixth Book of Moses called GOOD GOVERNMENT!" (The Primary Missing Book in the Holy Bible!) **By The Worldwide People's Revolution!®** Book 126.

{NOTE: That List of Available Books will be Updated, Periodically, if we do not get Killed by some Thugs, who Work for those Lying Conniving Edomites!}

The Enticement,

Our Selected King, is having Compassion on Humanity in this Special
Book, which Reveals HOW to Prevent the Common Cold, and HOW to
"Catch" the Common Cold, Guaranteed! In Fact, he Proves that we
EAT it, even as it is Revealed in *Numbers 11*, by Moses, himself.
Moreover, our Selected King also Reveals HOW to Overcome almost
all Sicknesses and Diseases, if anyone is Interested in it. Most Medical
Doctors are NOT: beCause all such Great Truths might Destroy their
Crafts, even as the Silversmiths were Threatened by the Great Truths
that were Taught by the Apostle Paul in *Acts 19*.